D1823665

CHRONICLES
of a
CORPORATE
HIPPY

"When change or die were the only options."

By Tim McMahon

~~~

...author's frank and candid reflection of his life will resonate with anyone embarking on a spiritual journey or questioning their lives...

S Perris. 40 – Phycologist - UK

...I completely got into the book and honestly it made me think ... Laugh ... Cry and that is what a good book is all about...

Mariselle F. 35 – Hotel Manager - South African.

...It might share a genre with Eat, Pray, Love, but all comparisons end there. McMahon's story is a wake-up call for the corporate drones of the West...

Jason L. 38 - Consultant, Trainer & Growth Hacker – USA.

...from Corporate Wage-Slave to Freewheeling Traveler is a rollercoaster of emotions and laughter...

Bev T. 46 – Marketing Manager – UK

...self-help served cold. A dark personal story of letting go in every sense possible. This book will make you cry, yearn and leave you at peace...

Eduardo C. 30 – Journalist – USA.

...I found it honest, heartfelt, funny, brash yet sensitive and damn genuine...

Angela A. 43 - Financial Planner – Australia

...brutally honest, it makes you wince at times! It asks questions most people are afraid to ask but are niggling us in the back of our mind...

John T. 55 – Life Coach - Australia

...light-hearted and at other times deeply troubling, the content is relatable and touches on aspects of human life that we all share...

Chris H. 35 - Photographer – Canada.

Join the movement!

Corporate Hippy
R-evolution

'Sharing Lessons Learned'
Awareness | Balance | Empowerment

The Mission

*"Influence and 'empower' people, executives and corporations
in making 'balanced' choices with 'awareness' for an improved and sustainable
life experience for One Million individuals by 2020."*

@ Facebook: Corporate Hippy R-evolution
www.facebook.com/groups/CorporateHippyRevolution

Get the Moaching and Courses: www.corporate-hippy.com

*"It doesn't matter how hard life punches you in the face,
I found it's what you do about it
that really counts."*

Tim McMahon.

In Loving Memory of:

Kevin Jonathan McMahon – RIP, 28th December 2006.
Julie Anne McMahon – RIP, 19th April 2010.

These people changed my life forever, they still inspire me every day
to put one foot in front of the other and keep on moving forward
with spirit and gratitude.

*"Finally an authentic, raw and at times funny,
true story of a 40-something ex-corporate guy finding
'meaning'
through adventurous travels."*

CHRONICLES
of a
CORPORATE
HIPPY

"When change or die were the only options."

.

By Tim McMahon

**25% of author's profits are donated to grassroots
charities.**

Edited by: Wayne Duckworth
Cover Design by: Shawn Fredrick Muller

Published by: Tim McMahon
www.corporate-hippy.com

TABLE CONTENTS

ACKNOWLEDGEMENT

These people have impacted my life experience on this crazy planet in so many different ways. If it were not for them doing their bad, good or indifferent, I would not be who or where I am today. Reflecting on the past and the situations I found myself in, these people all made a lasting impression on my life… I can see this now as a positive and I am forever thankful for crossing their paths.

I believe when one does me wrong, or I think they have, I can view this as a lesson in life to wake me up. The other is my own flaws and sure as shit I had, have and no doubt will discover more in time, like I recently did.

So, I want to take the time to wholeheartedly thank these people for coming into my life and helping me wake up and find my way.

Kevin Jonathan McMahon, Julie Anne McMahon, my little sister and older brother, Mr. Minister, Smiling-Assassin, Bald-Ego, Dog-Man, Guru-Guy, Coach-Guy, Doc-B, Flat Mate, Little-Guy, The-Kid, Coke-up Stalker, Gorilla-Agent, Aussie Paralytic Team, BSMF, DRC Military, Old Man America, Mucho Aussie Guy, Bookworm Girl, Miss America, Jungle Guides and Divine Joe.

To the people and 'characters', I am forever grateful for meeting you and more importantly the lessons.

Special acknowledgement for their guidance and support:

James Mortimer-Roberts
Wayne Duckworth

INTRODUCTION

By – Tim McMahon

C hronicles of a Corporate Hippy is a raw, humorous and heartfelt account of living and trying to cope in the 21st Century and surviving it relatively sane. It covers some tough subjects that are commonly ignored due to fear such as depression, death, suicide and breaking free from the common and expected way of living that we all seem to hold onto so damn tightly.

The Chronicles stretches over a four-year period, taking you on a brutal and emotional roller coaster ride through the darkest experiences of being a human. However, it gives you hope: there is always an option to change and live a more satisfying life if you're prepared to be aware of and listen to your inner voice telling you that you do in fact have many choices and can change.

The WHY?

"I may have something within me of value, maybe not just to me"
Maya Angelou

There are many reasons why I wrote this book, one being just the challenge of writing a book since I failed every single English exam I took at school and I can't spell to save my life… I won't even mention grammar or punctuation.

The other reasons are vast, so here I go with just a few… I was thinking it's time that I spoke my truth, tell others from my perspective the life experiences I was having and how they impacted me and more importantly, how I overcame them. I started to believe that what I had experienced and learnt could assist others and at some stage maybe even change the way we all operate as people.

I became aware I could hold onto what I had learnt and be somewhat selfish or pay it forward in a way that was authentic and real. I wrote most of the book from that little voice in my head that we all have, the voice that most of the time is not heard by others due to its shocking honesty. I wanted to show that a grown man can be vulnerable with his words and be totally ok with it, if not empowered. This may lead to others speaking their truth and being vulnerable – not weak but vulnerable. I learnt there is a massive difference… *who would have thought?*

So, the book is written as an example that it's totally fine to be authentic and or vulnerable with yourself and others. I believe the more you are, the better the life you live, regardless if you have to face the 'tough shit' that comes up from time to time.

The last 'why' of writing the book was to share my story, my pain and my triumphs with others and to see the look in their eyes of… *Holy shit, you too!* It just makes the journey that much sweeter to know we are essentially all in this together, regardless of who we think we are, where we are from or what we do.

CHAPTER 1:
HOW LITTLE DID I KNOW...

You know how a specific date sticks in your head? A date that reminds you of your past – the good, the bad and the amazing times life dishes out?

One of those dates is the 28th of December 2006. The morning of that day was the start of a very painful, eye-opening and amazing journey into death, travel and life. All I can say is: how little did I know what was about to unfold.

The morning of the 28th I was fast asleep, enjoying the wonders of dream-land (and damn I love sleep) when my roommate burst into my room. It was frickin' four thirty a.m. He was holding the phone with a look of utter shock and disbelief on his face. Being very cool and all, I was sleeping naked and completely uncovered. Realizing my roommate had just noticed I was totally naked too, I was still not entirely sure that this was the reason for his utterly shocked look. And what the hell was he doing in my room at four thirty in the morning holding the phone anyways?

Life was about to unleash a very cruel punch and then continue to rip the arms and legs off me for some time to come.

I covered myself up and my roommate handed me the phone. Oh, what a surprise, it was my mother. *Great.* Normally it was the police calling me to ask me to pick up my little brother Kev, who had been having a few issues with authority and life over the past, well, several years.

What the hell was she calling me for at this time in the morning? *This had better be good.*

At first it was hard to work out what the hell she was saying. She was going completely crazy on the phone, crying in hysterics about something. I asked her to calm down, told her it would all be ok. I was thinking, *lady just relax, it can't be that bad.* Then I finally worked out what she was saying and damn. Those words. Those words were about to turn my whole life on its ass.

Still in complete hysterics, Mum managed to piece together the sentence, "I have the police here, Kevin has committed suicide… he is dead."

What the fuck? No he isn't. Is he? My brain felt like it had frozen and then blown a fuse. I had been kind of waiting for this.

And she just kept on repeating, "Kevin is dead," over and over again, sobbing uncontrollably until it started to sink in. Well just a bit, anyways.

He had gone out the night before, a Wednesday night, and got very drunk out of his mind and decided to throw himself in front of a train at around one thirty in the morning. He was killed instantly, at only seventeen years old.

Kev was the type of young guy that most people liked or loved. He was a special soul. We were very close and spent a lot of time together hanging out. I just *got* him. He was intensely emotional and sensitive; a creative guy with a wealth of talent for music and the arts. Yet he struggled greatly with the demands of life.

Tall, skinny and awkward with dyed black hair (Goth phase), he had very kind eyes and fair skin, and such a great sense of humor. He loved a good laugh. He was one of those people who tried so hard to do the right thing, yet messed up regularly. He would get very disappointed and angry with himself, along with pissing people off around him. During this time of his life, he was messed up.

Sitting there on my bed, my head was spinning totally out of control. Added to that, I was hot and then had cold clammy sweats. My whole world had come to a neck-breaking stop.

There was complete silence, just a ringing sound which felt like it went on for hours as my mind raced through thousands of memories of Kev, with the final one of him being in bed asleep. This was a weird-ass dream I was having. *Please, please, please, this has to be a dream,* I was thinking (or more hoping).

Realizing Mum was still on the phone in hysterics, the idea that my little brother was dead – gone – had killed himself – was hard to get my head around at 4.30 a.m. My first reaction was to pick up my mobile and call him to see if he was ok or if he needed some help. *No phones in heaven, I guess.*

The crazy shit you think of in moments of disbelief.

I continued talking with Mum, trying to comfort her as much as possible as I felt my world inch by inch coming down around me. Finally, we agreed that I would call my older brother and my younger sister – I'm the middle child, lucky me – with the new family news of the day in hand. Or that should be, really early morning news. *Great.* Just what I like doing at four thirty in the bloody morning: calling around telling people that there has been a suicide in the family.

I hung up from Mum. My heart racing, thoughts all over the place, I was sweating and barely breathing. I leant across to the bedside table and picked up my mobile and for some reason I started to dial Kev's number. I'm not sure why. But thinking maybe this was all a bad messed-up dream, I was in some kind of alternative universe. *He's still alive and well, I should tell him the news too.*

I just wanted to communicate with him to make sure he was ok; tell him it was going to work out and everything was going to be fine.

It was so confusing how just yesterday afternoon he had been standing right in front of me and I was saying goodbye to him, telling him I loved him and I would see him soon. This was after dropping him home from Christmas celebrations which had happened to drag out far too long.

The crazy thing was I could remember seeing him out of the corner of my eye as I drove off and a small but faint thought gently flowed through my mind. *Tim, you will not see him again alive.* At the time, I chose not to listen to it and just thought I should cut back on drinking.

While I was deep inside my own head, my poor roommate was still standing in the doorway to my bedroom in total shock. He and Kev were very close, as he used to help me out with Kev when needed – and at times it *was* needed. It had been an interesting twenty-four months with a seventeen-year-old trying to find his way in the world and making a lot of mistakes – drinking, drugs and loads of trouble with the police.

I got dressed, my head still spinning out of control. I felt so totally numb. The realization of the enormous loss was starting to creep into my mind, my body and my soul. Loss is one emotion that does my head in and I have no idea how to understand it, nor deal with it. Normally I run. Fast.

I have been in this shitty situation a few times before, with my father dying when I was fourteen and my beautiful and inspiring grandmother dying some ten years later. I have no idea how to deal with the death of someone I love. The pain was fuckin' unbearable.

It was five o'clock in the morning and I was trying to get my head together to call my sister, knowing that not only was she was seven months pregnant and a little unstable, but had had some past issues with Kev. Damn, I could think of so many other things that I would rather be doing – like sleeping – going back into my dreamland where everything would be great, fuzzy and warm.

What the hell would I say? How the hell do you tell someone horrific news like that? I sat there for a while, thoughts running through my head.

Hi, it's Tim, yes I know it's early but I need to tell you that Kev threw himself in front of a train, is in many pieces and is dead. Have a nice day…

What the hell? Thinking, thinking, thinking… And feeling I was starting to freak out and over-analyze it.

I decided I would just call and say it how it was.

Dialing the number, my body was not reacting well – clammy cold sweats had started up again, my heart felt like it was beating itself to death and my mind was totally out of control.

Why the hell did I agree to do this?

My sister answered and not very welcomingly at all. No surprise really. So, I took a deep breath and just said it how it was. "Hey love, Mum just called me and unfortunately, Kev killed himself last night; he threw himself in front of a train." Then I breathed out. Complete silence. More silence. *Total* silence. Then finally some noise: a groan of overwhelming emotional confusion and disapproval of what she had just been told.

The response was not a good one – it didn't help that she'd never been a morning person. We talked further briefly; hearing the complete and utter painful disbelief in her voice, the fight for non-acceptance started within me. The realization process kicked in. I guess the more you talk about something the more it starts to live within your mind or your reality.

Then I called my older brother. He was down the coast for the Christmas holidays with his family, at the place the whole family had been going for the past forty years and where we had all planned to be this year to enjoy another family holiday together by the beach.

He finally answered the phone and I repeated to him the news of Kev and what had happened, trying to spare too much detail. I told him that we would all meet at Mum's house to… *Hmmm… Well… To do what?* I guess just all come together as a family and get our heads around what had just happened. Again, I heard the non-acceptance and overwhelming disbelief in my older brother's voice.

"Oh no, oh no, oh no, Kev what have you done?" The whole situation was becoming more in-my-face reality. Hate reality. Much prefer the wonders of warm, fuzzy, dreamland.

The more I fight reality, the less painful this will be, I thought. The realization that my little brother – my best mate, was dead and I could not help him or protect him anymore, that felt like someone had ripping out all the goodness and happiness within me. It was the total loss of anything good in life.

How do I go forward from that?

Having finally completed the onerous duty of calling around to let people know that my little brother was dead, having killed himself, it was time for a coffee and smoke: my thinking time.

Sitting on the front balcony overlooking the street with the sun slowly rising, I tried to reconcile my thoughts with what the hell was going on. *What was life all about? Why are we all here? What the hell am I doing?* Thinking, thinking, thinking, some more thinking. Then... screech... STOP THINKING!

The weirdest thoughts started flowing into my head. *Mum should have been the next to die, not Kev.*

Mum had terminal cancer and in my mind, or my skewed expectations, she was next to die. That's how it would roll, not Kev, who to me was like a son and a little brother all rolled up into one amazingly talented, loving, funny guy. *What the hell do I do now?*

What I had expected in life and my ideas about the way things were going to develop had just changed forever. My ability to manage my life expectations was, somewhat, unstable.

Winding the clock back for a moment, Kev's issues had started about two years back when he and Mum had had a major falling out (no, not your normal type of family falling out) to the point where Mum had the police charge Kev with assault. *Nice one Mum.* It was over some goings-on in the car on the way to music practice. *As one would think.*

Kev and Mum were doing their normal thing of fighting and Kev, being a smart-ass, decided to grab the steering wheel of the car to freak Mum out. And Mum *totally* freaked out, grabbed his fingers and bent them back, badly breaking two. Kev in his pain turned and bit Mum on the upper arm (as you do in those situations) in the hope she would let go. In his pain and struggle to free himself from Mum's grip, he managed to smash the windscreen with his feet.

Whatever happened to talking things through guys? *Come on!*

So, that was the end of 'happy families' as we knew it and that's when I stepped into see what I could do. As I said, Kev was like a best mate, a son and my little brother all rolled up into one person. We had a very strong connection, a great relationship and we spent a lot of time together. I guess you could loosely call me a 'father figure' to him. *Hmmm… Well maybe.*

So, after all this drama, and with me clearly having no idea about what had just gone on, I received the motherly phone call and the full story of "just another drama" in our family. The story finished with how Kev had moved out and she was not sure where he was.

A little "Magnum PI" work on my part managed to get me in contact with him. We decided to meet up for lunch and try to work out what to do and how I could help him out, me being the father figure and all…

Seeing this poor, skinny fifteen-year-old kid dragging his ass up the street was heart breaking to say the least, but to see the extent of his injuries was horrifying. The old girl *Mum* still had some fight left in her; she was struggling with her cancer and battling on.

Little did I know that life was readying itself to dish out more fun and games.

Kev and I had lunch and talked about everything that had gone on in the car and with Mum. We also talked about where he was living and with whom, and sorted out a time to go meet with them to see what we could all do to help him out.

Meanwhile all the bullshit with the court case Mum had brought against Kev was going on in the background with the lawyers and what not. I was requested to be in court with my little brother, versus my mother. A classic *WTF?* Moment. Honestly, it was a total waste of everyone's time and the case was resolved in about ten minutes. Bam... done! Happy families again. Unfortunately, Kev did not want to have anything to do with Mum for quite some time.

Next step was getting my little brother sorted out with accommodation, schooling, food and all the crap a fifteen-year-old thinks is, "like", important.

Over the following few months and after seeing many youth accommodation options, I managed to get Kev into a reasonable place for kids under eighteen. But I tell you, it was a hard road trying to work out the good from the bad, since most of the places seemed to be the same. Honestly there were some scary places: borderline prisons in the suburbs for youths with nowhere to go.

While the whole under-eighteens-*prison*-accommodation-search was going on, Kev was living with me and, *holy shit*. Living with a fifteen-year-old, you start to understand what goes on in the heads of the youths of today.

It was mind-boggling! Sleeping, eating, playing computer games, eating, sleeping more. And, much to my surprise, waxing their legs because they're bored. Apparently, hair on legs is, "like, so uncool." Just another amazing *what-the-fuck?* Moment.

Having said that however, this kid had so many amazing talents for music and art it was incredible. If *only, if* only, he was still here to explore those talents.

I did a deal with Kev: if he went to school and did the right thing, he could live with me for three to six months. All agreed and all good. That lasted for about two weeks until I found out that he was not going to school, he refused to pay for anything and that he had come very close to burning down my house. The thing was he was getting money from the government weekly for schooling because he was not living with Mum, yet he decided to invest the money in buying crap.

Crunch time! Honestly, those were some of the hardest things I have ever done: not only living with a fifteen-year-old, but trying to enforce a line that he had stepped over repeatedly. He had broken our deal many a time, so I kicked him out. *Back on the streets young man you go.*

I was sure I was doing the right thing for him and me in the long term but watching him walk out of my place and down the street with one small bag and a garbage bag full of his worldly possessions just ripped my heart out, I felt like a totally insensitive douche bag. I never knew if I was doing the right thing. How could I know? I was merely a single guy, with little-to-no parenting skills and an intense career in corporate IT sales. I had twenty-four hours a day of corporate crap – boy's club bullshit – and I was stressed out of my brain.

After a few hours, damn it, I gave in and went and found him. We had it out and made another deal for him to stay with me. Clearly, what I did had freaked him out (got to love the no-bullshit policy) as he was more understanding and accepting of what he had to do now, thank God.

In the end, I finally found a brilliant organization that would help Kev and me out. It was like a halfway house for lost youths in the area; the people running it were amazing and very helpful. I'm forever grateful to them for helping me out and more importantly, for helping Kev.

A few months later… We, 'as a family', had planned a trip to Thailand to just relax, have some fun and enjoy our time with each other. This was when things for me started to change. I became very aware things were not quite right with Kev emotionally.

We managed to have some amazing times until things went a little wrong. Kev was out at night, getting drunk and going crazy, which is fine if you're eighteen plus and have the mentality to deal with it. But Kev was born nearly three months prematurely and suffered from hydrocephalus. The outcome of this was that parts of his frontal lobes were not formed properly, affecting his moods and how he processed thoughts and feelings, although he was a completely normal person (if there is such a thing).

The reason I know all this was because when Mum was in hospital trying to die of cancer (this was not the first – more on that later) I was running around taking Kev to crazy head doctors so they could try what seemed like any or every mood-altering drug on him with little, if any thought to how it was affecting him. This meant: two to three different types of mood-altering drugs in a space of three to six months.

Seriously doctors, get your shit together. I know for a fact, from suffering from mental health challenges like anxiety and depression, the body and brain take around two to three months to adjust to these types of meds. Good news is that I am off the crazy pills now and I'm living a good life.

So, with all of this, Kev had a major meltdown while in Thailand, and it was at least fortunate that I could be there with him when it happened. What came out of it was truly heart wrenching.

I walked into the hotel room just before dinner and found Kev lying in bed staring at the ceiling, with a look of total despair on his face. I sat down with him, knowing things were not good. Kev was a very sensitive and emotional kid, and had experienced much suffering and bullying due to his condition.

He was in so much emotional pain, totally lost and feeling completely unwanted and unloved – his words. He went on to tell me, with tears rolling down his face that he felt he did not belong anywhere and did not feel part of the family. My heart truly hurt for him and I could feel his pain – I too at times felt the same feelings of being unloved and unwanted. I could totally understand where he was at. I told him, "Kev mate, I love you so much and you are so, so, so important to me and the family. You're an incredible person and we chose you to be in our lives – you're my brother, my best little mate, regardless of where you came from."

Kev had been adopted. The poor little guy just cried and cried and cried. We continued to talk for a while. However, being a little psychic and all, I could see this was the start of a steep and very slippery road for all involved.

Over the next few months leading up to Christmas, I did everything in my power to help, guide and assist Kev, but it was clearly not enough. It did not seem to matter what I did – or anyone else, for that matter. It felt like I was witnessing a massive train wreck, standing there on the sidelines, totally hopeless, with no power to change the situation. As I watched it unfold in real time, I knew the outcome would be cruel and painful for all – and it was. It ended on the morning of the 28th December 2006.

Yet again *how little did I know* what was to unravel in my life in the coming weeks and months…

ЖЖЖ

LESSONS LEARNT: #1

"When I realized that I could lose a loved one in the next second, minute, day, week or month.

I relaxed a little and let go, in the understanding of appreciating them just as they are in the present moment.

This was a massive game changer for me, leading to richer relationships without attachment to, the what if's and could be's."

CHAPTER 2

FACING THE REALITIES OF SUICIDE.

While sitting at my mother's house with the rest of the family, the police called to advise us that a family member was required to identify Kev's body at the mortuary. Just the thought of this churned my stomach to the point of vomiting – let alone actually witnessing the horrific sight of my little brother dead, lying on a table in pieces.

What I experienced with Kev's suicide is this: regardless of whatever happens, life still just rolls on. There are people to see, meals to prepare, corporate commitments to fulfill and bills to pay. Oh, and then there's attending the mortuary to identify your little brother's smashed up body.

But after much discussion with the family and given that my sister was seven months pregnant, my mother an emotional mess and my older brother at the time busy with work and family commitments (but did offer to attend), I thought *fuck it*. Considering I was the closest to him and had been with him for most of his ups and downs, this would be the right thing for me to do. And somewhere in my head I was thinking it would give me some kind of closure.

Damn, sometimes I wish I could think things through a little better.

I remember it was a Monday morning when I drove over to the mortuary with my roommate for moral support. We chatted nervously about general bullshit stuff on the way until I turned down the street to the mortuary and truly began to freak out, not knowing what I was about to witness. Would I be able to recognize Kev? Were his arms and legs still attached? And what about his face…? *Oh, his face…did the train smash his face apart too?*

My head started spinning totally out of control with thoughts and images of Kev's poor little seventeen-year-old body lying there. *Would there still be blood all over him?* Holy shit what the hell was I doing? *Damn, fuck, fuck shit…* I could have been at the beach or hanging with friends having brunch. Now my stomach was churning tenfold and all I could think was… *WTF!*

What happens if I get in there and vomit all over him? Why am I doing this? I kept asking myself this over and over and over again.

This was all going on in my head while I was attempting to park the car. Then my thoughts suddenly stopped and for a split second my mind zoomed back a few years. Ironically, the mortuary was a familiar place to me. About five years back before I went travelling to South America, I had helped out a friend who owned a funeral home. The crazy shit you do for friends or for that little extra holiday-spending money!

The last time I was there, I had to pick up the body of a little old lady to take back to the funeral home. While trying to get her out of the mortuary freezer and into the van we had the misfortune of getting her arm stuck in the door of the freezer. At the time, I was completely freaked out, fearing we would snap it off. *How the hell do you explain that?* It was such a surreal situation; never in a million years did I imagine I would be back here at the mortuary to identify my little brother's body. The things that life throws at you…

Having a little nervous chuckle to myself about the arm-stuck-in-the-freezer-door memory, I realized my emotions and my mind were like a blender with the lid off: *shit was flying everywhere.* I just needed to focus on the job at hand and my roommate was looking at me, clearly thinking, what the hell is going on in his head? I had no idea.

In a complete daze, I got out of the car and walked across the street and up the stairs to the mortuary entrance. My legs were shaking and still my bloody stomach was churning itself to pieces. At this point I was so sure I was going to vomit. Opening the door to the mortuary's office, I was overcome with the intense smell of death, slapping me in the face like an old dead fish – rather sobering, to say the least.

The freakiest thing at this point was the massive tall creepy guy at the services counter who just stood there staring at me. I started staring back at him. *Is this guy alive or dead? Have I walked into an alternative zombie universe and come face-to-face with some human-zombie-clone?*

A short conversation with him reassured me that he was in fact alive and actually quite nice. I guessed his chosen career might have affected him somewhat.

I completed all the paperwork and was guided into an extremely well lit, small, cold and very white room. I was looking down at the ground and completely 'in my head' with thoughts of anything and everything flying around like a high speed merry-go-around – but not very frickin' merry. Then the creepy guy said, "I will leave you alone for a moment." Somewhere in that creepy deep voice, however, there was a hint of compassion... nice.

The door slowly shut, finishing up with a bang. That really unsettled me. I was now alone in the bright little room, with my dead brother lying on a table about a meter away. *What the hell am I doing there?*

I took a great big deep breath – not such a good idea at the time as the smell of the embalming fluid was thick in the air. My heart was racing and I was having that filthy hot and cold clammy, sweating feeling again. My mouth was dry; like I had been licking the carpet at the local nightclub. I stopped, gathered myself together and then I looked up. Right in front of me was what was left of my amazingly talented and kind-hearted little brother. My heart felt like it fell out of my ass and onto the floor while simultaneously pushing up and out of my throat and choking me. I could barely breathe.

Standing there looking at Kev with his little broken face poking out of a white sheet that was covering the rest of his body, all I could think was, *Oh you silly, silly, silly, boy Kev.* I felt so much love for him and all I wanted to do was give him the biggest loving and most truthful hug I could give. You see that stuff in movies when someone has died and *WOW* what a beautiful last thing to do, hug your loved one for the very last time. If only this had been movie.

I leant forward towards Kev with an open heart, great love and good intentions…. *Holy shit!* At closer inspection, his head was way out of shape. A small stream of fluid was leaking from his right eye and another from the corner of his mouth. I took a very quick step back in fear that I was going to totally lose my shit and vomit all over him. It took all that I had to gather myself together. Giving myself some space to view Kev from a distance, a total calmness overcame me; a stillness. I was able to stand there and look death in the face and for a moment experience what death was in another: a shell of a seventeen-year-old human who had – no spirit – who had long gone.

That was enough for me for one day. I said one last good bye to Kev – or at least the shell of Kev on this earth anyway. The interesting thing about viewing a dead body is it looks a little plastic or rubbery, like if you dropped it on the floor, it would bounce back up and hit the roof.

I said a quick thank you to the creepy tall guy, signed another document and got the hell out of there. Leaving the mortuary, I thought that would be the last time I would see Kev in human form.

Ж Ж Ж

CHAPTER 3:
FAMILY AND FUNERALS.

L ife was still going on and it was funeral planning day involving the family, the minister and the funeral people. At the time, I was thinking it should be basically an open and shut case. I knew what I wanted and how I wanted to be involved. That was to do a speech about Kev and his amazingly colorful life, then say the final goodbyes, and play just one song: ColdPlay, X &Y track 4, Fix You. That was it – no more, no less. (I was trying so hard to rush the grieving process and get on with life - closure, closure, closure!)

Well do you think it could be that easy? Of course not. For God's sake, I had looked after and supported Kev for the past few years like he was my own son; I had been to hell and back with him on the emotional roller coaster with alcohol and drug abuse, depression and the 2 a.m. calls from the police asking me to pick him up. Plus, I'd been doing my twenty-four-hours-a-day career bullshit, studying and trying to have a normal life whilst fitting in my own drug and alcohol abuse.

It turns out that what I wanted was not important and what I said was not heard. Furthermore, if I wanted to read out my final goodbyes in church, the minister had to pre-approve it. WTF? It was not a frickin' home loan, it was an emotional heart-driven goodbye letter to my little brother.

I was sitting there listening to everyone go on about Kev and how they wanted the funeral to go and I was starting to think, *this is all too damn hard. I'm so out of here. And they can shove the funeral affair up their asses.* Yes, I was a little emotional. Furthermore, I had, had a massive realization earlier that morning: helping and supporting Kev had given me meaning in my life and now I had lost Kev and my primary purpose had gone too. Realizing this had really stopped me dead in my tracks, another large smack in the face from life. My life was coming apart at a rate of knots with that nice, sinking feeling of being in deep, deep in trouble and totally lost. *What the hell would I do next?*

In the discussion that was being had, I felt I was not being heard nor taken seriously. And there's nothing worse than telling people things that are super emotionally important to you and them looking at you and smiling like you're some lost, purposeless freak. Well, I ended up losing my shit and saying it how felt and they all finally got the message loud and clear.

God love my little sister, she backed me up. Mr. Minister didn't look too happy and never made eye contact with me again. But with no pre-approval required for speaking in church, the family went on their merry way, and the funeral was sorted out.

Suddenly it was the morning of the funeral. *Great.* I had been dreading this day. How was it all going to work? What was going to happen? Would I hold my shit together and not lose it in front of others, avoiding looking like a complete and total dickhead? *Hmmm…* The thought of facing all those people – family, friends, old friends, work colleagues turning up to show their respects – was more than I could face. And what the hell do you wear to a funeral? *Black?*

I just felt like curling up and hiding under a big old rock or sitting at home smoking myself stupid and drinking far too much coffee till my brain exploded. But there was another surprise to come: the family had agreed to have a final viewing of Kev at the funeral home. Guess I had missed that family meeting. Feeling very fucked up and lost I decided it was best I attended; no energy to fight, just flow with it. I'm saying my final goodbyes to Kev and my primary purpose in life (this did come back to smack me in the face hard – wish I knew then what I would come to know about the importance of one's purpose in life). So, that's the focus of the day ahead: view dead brother, go to dead brother's funeral, go to dead brother's wake, go home and cry… Busy day.

First it was meeting the family at Mum's house. And more family. And friends. And old friends. And people from overseas. People everywhere – popping out of the frickin' woodwork. This was so the last thing on earth that I wanted to be doing, but I was trapped in the ever moving 'funeral process' and there was no turning back. Next stop: funeral home, and I get to see my little brother all put back together again in a nice white box.

The crazy thoughts started up again. *Ok, so I saw him alive a week or so before I saw him munched up in the mortuary, and now I am going to see him again munched up but somewhat rebuilt, maybe with make up on, like they did at the funeral home I helped out in a few years back. Can I do this?*

All would be ok I kept telling myself, but then I thought, He will look so weird with make-up on, and my head just went mental, spitting out so much crap, what-if's, and more crap. *When will my head, mind, thoughts stop? Give me a break!*

Ok, I had made it to the funeral home. Some family and a few close friends were there. It was a weird-ass funeral home: not so classy, very cheap and 1980's looking, beige everywhere, with that nice, musty damp smell.

Looking around I turned to see in the far-left corner a large white box on a stand with flowers around it. *I guess this is Kev's vessel* to the other world. In the background, I could hear cheesy, heart wrenching and depressing music playing as I slowly walked closer to the large white box where my little brother lay. A family member was leaning over the white box muttering some words. I started to think, *What the hell are they saying and hmmm… What does Kev look like?*

A cold chill ran through me and a quick flashback of Kev appeared of when I last saw him alive – it had been about ten days ago, when I had dropped him back at this house. Next up, he was lying in the mortuary all smashed up with his little face poking out from the white sheet and fluid leaking from his right eye and the corner of his mouth. Suddenly all my thoughts stopped and I lost my breath for a moment. A loud and clear thought appeared. *Is this a good idea to see him again?*

Too late now! It was my turn to view him.

Do I want to do this? No, I wanted to run and run fast. For some reason, however, I slowly walked up to the white box and gently leant over to look in. My heart was pounding like it was going to pop out of my chest and join Kev in the white box, I had no idea what to do or say and I stood there like a stunned mullet staring in disbelief. They had put my little brother back together again. It was quite amazing – he looked alive, like he was playing dead and at any moment he was going to burst out laughing and scare the shit out of me. That was one of his things he would do, hide somewhere in my house and jump out, scaring me stupid.

I stood there staring at Kev's reconstructed, lifeless body for what seemed like hours, I felt so numb and stunned like I had just been tasered in the face. I was totally out of my depth to even consider dealing with something like this. *What the hell was I doing to myself?* I realized right then that viewing Kev's body right then for the final time was going to haunt the hell out of me for years to come.

It's confronting to see someone who you love so much, alive and healthy one week, then dead and smashed up in a mortuary the next, then a few days later beautifully put back together again like nothing had ever happened. Yet he is still dead.

Why? What? Damn! What do you do with that?

Leaving the funeral home, I was totally confused, my emotions running wild, trying to process seeing Kev all put back to together again like Humpty Dumpty. This would be the last time I would see Kev in his human form, yet etched in my mind were the three different states I had seen him in… *Head-fuck anyone?*

The plan was to meet some family and close friends at a cafe near the church and wait for the funeral to start, which was about an hour's time away. Sitting at the cafe, located across the road from the train station, I sat there drinking my coffee and smoking as everyone around me was talking. I have no idea what they were saying and more to the point I did not give a shit. I was busy in my head thinking about what was to come with the funeral.

Would I hold my shit together? Who would be there? Who else do I have to face today?

So many questions. All I wanted was for this to stop. I wanted life to stop, I wanted to get off the bus – so to speak – run, and just keep running. Life was not meant to go this way; this shit happens to other people and you read about this stuff in newspapers or hear stories of how someone's brother or kid killed himself. *This is not my life and this just can't be happening.* I was getting more and more upset and anxious – it felt like I was going to explode and implode all at the same time.

Staring out into nowhere-land with the faint sound of chatter in the background, I looked over to the train station to see a myriad of Goth-type teenagers all in black with standard Goth war-paint. Black eyes, black lips and painted fingernails, complete with dyed black hair, and all holding a single long-stemmed sunflower. It was like a single file of little worker ants streaming out of the train station, through the gates and up the road, making their way towards the church. They were all Kev's friends. Good old Kev had been through a crazy-assed

Goth phase. That was an interesting time, to say the least.

Thinking back to his Goth stage, it was a time when I had to just accept him for what he was and understand that it was just a phase and, if I was in public, not give a shit what others thought or said. Surprising what you do when you love and accept someone: you don't give a shit what they look like, nor what they wear. Which reminds me of a classic Kev moment.

I had met Kev for dinner one night after work and he was dressed in all his Goth war paint and black clothes, with a stylish black leather jacket. We walked into an upmarket restaurant, mostly filled with older, uptight-looking people – we were in an expensive area of Sydney. They were all looking at Kev and me, as I was dressed in a very much contrasting designer suit, tie, jacket and shiny shoes – living the corporate life.

What a sight we were. Kev took his black leather jacket off and sat down at the table. This was when I noticed that more and more people were staring and they were getting very upset. *Hmmm… What the hell is going on?* Then Kev got up to go to the toilet and *oh my god* on the back of his T-shirt were the words "Jesus is a Cunt." I sat there stunned with everyone staring at me. Only God knows what they were thinking. I got Kev to put his jacket back on and we both quickly ate dinner and got out of there. *Nice one Kev…* Yet that was who he was.

ЖЖЖ

CHAPTER 4

FINAL GOODBYES.

I arrived at the church thinking, *Last time I was here was for my little sister's wedding and now we are all here for my little brother's funeral.* Weird as it may sound, most of the same people were at both – not counting the Goth brigade. Interesting how you can see the same people altogether at a wedding and a funeral. Walking into the church, I remembered it being a lot bigger and less dark for my sister's wedding. And it too had that same musty damp smell of the funeral home.

Walking down the aisle with the large white box with flowers all over it, I took my seat and picked up what I guess is called the 'funeral information card' – just like the safety card on a plane. However, this one had no directions to the emergency exits or any instructions on how to put on the life jacket. Right then and there, what I needed was a life jacket because I was sinking, and sinking fast. My heart was pounding deeply, my head felt like it was about to explode and I was choking back my emotions. This was all so, so, wrong. *Reality check please?*

The 'funeral process' started moving along as planned, like some type of Broadway show: music, singing and Bible readings, minus the dancing girls, but all very well-choreographed. I was sitting there completely alone, when I heard my name being called, "Tim, Tim… Tim…"

Oh, shit I have to get up there and read my final "non-pre-approved" letter. Mr. Minister was standing there looking at me. *FUCK! Abort, abort, abort!*

Bizarrely, I couldn't even think yet, though I knew I had to read out a heart-felt letter in front of all those people. *What the hell was I thinking?*

I was so deep in the "funeral process" I couldn't pull out now or it would wreck the "show." And the show must go on. I stood up slowly, shaking like a crazy man on acid and walked over to the microphone, trying not to trip on the step and push over the white box. I stood there and looked out towards all the people paying their respects to Kev and, *holy shit the church was packed…* Standing room only.

I pulled out my letter with everyone in the church looking at me. *Argh, the pressure.* And right then, time stood still for one peaceful moment. There was nothingness: just a church packed with people staring at me. I guessed they were all wondering what the hell I was about to do. (I had an undesirable history with the family and some of my mother's close friends.) I could feel Mr. Minister's eyes on me, just waiting for me to trip up.

I took a big, deep breath and slowly let the air out, got my head together and this is what I read…

To My Little Mate,

It's hard to believe that you're gone so soon, I know how hard you found living your life. I understand and accept your choice to check out to find peace in your life, a place where you could be truly you and free!

I love you and respect you for that!

We worked so hard together to make things right, happy, fun and enjoyable! I know that you were trying your heart out and giving it all you had and all you wanted from the world was to be just you and that that would be OK.

To me, you were just so perfect being you and I am so, so proud of you and what you have achieved; it fills my heart with happiness that you did so much and so well.

Kevy, you are the most kind-hearted, amazing, unique and talented person I have ever known, with the things you said and the things you have done and could do! In my eyes you are the bestest little bro and little mate any big brother or mate could have ever asked for …… by far!

Now that you have gone to a better place I can only think of all the amazing, fun and dumb-ass times we had together: our road trips, chats on MSN, Thailand and our interesting day trip to Phuket city –ick! And most of all, the times you would visit for dinner or to just hang out and you running around the house scaring the shit out of Aunty Pete and me. Ya cheeky bugger!

Kevy, I am going to miss you so, so very much, I wish I could be there with you now, but I have many things that I want to do and finish here first, but before you know it I will be there with you having a drink and a good old family ciggy and of course a giggle!

Thanks so much for your friendship and love and the incredible journey we had, you will always be in my heart!

It's time to say bye, see ya soon and you make sure you save me a seat right next to you.

Lov ya long time little mate!

Ps. We got ya a lovely white vessel for your next journey and I must say it's very you…. lov ya!

…

Thank God that is over. I stumbled back to my seat and sat down. Then the music started to play and it was time to get on with the show. The family was asked to stand by the large white box for the final, final, final goodbyes. *Really?* I had said so many goodbyes it was starting to hurt my head.

Right on cue ColdPlay's *Fix You* started playing loud and clear throughout the musty smelling, dark and ever-shrinking church; I was starting to suffocate. Resting my hand on the large white box where my little brother lay, the overwhelming pain and loss was being driven home like a massive rusty nail slowly being pounded into my heart.

At this point I could not breathe. My body had seized up and my heart was pounding so hard and deep I could barely stand… I was about to have a bloody heart attack when the funeral showgirls grabbed the white box and slowly walked out of the church, as everyone stood, stared, cried, and I guess, said their own goodbyes as well. This was truly a very screwed up situation to be present in.

Trying to pull myself together, placing my sunglasses on, I could hardly see anything, and more to the point, I didn't want to. I slowly walked down the aisle with my family out into the bright, hot, sunny light of a beautiful day. *Seriously!* It would have been so much better for it to have been a cold, raining day, to match what I was feeling.

Standing outside for one split second, I was in a lather of sweat with tears rolling down my face and a real snotty nose. I just wanted to drop dead right where I stood. My boss's wife grabbed my arm and I looked at her; tears running down her face too. She told me how beautiful the service was and how she would like to have dinner soon to hear more about Kev and his funny stories. She thought Kev had a very fascinating life and wanted to learn more. I just stared at her blankly and said "Ok", "lovely and thank you." I knew full well this dinner would never happen.

People say nice shit at funerals; they get carried away with all the emotions and the "funeral process" stuff, and never follow up on their promises. A few hours or a day later, life is all great, fine and normal for them. Yet I still have to deal with the loss, grief and the reality that a loved one is gone. For me that meant also trying to face the fact that Kev had killed himself, along with my primary purpose in life.

What do I do next and how does anyone move forward from this?

...

So, with the funeral out of the way, it was time to hang out with more people back at my mum's house: a kind of wake thingy that the family thought would be a great idea. *Really? I so don't want to face any more people, family or friends at this stage.* I wished everyone would just piss off and leave me alone. Especially those I had never met before in my life. You know, the kind who want to talk to you and add some dumb-ass positive comment right at the moment you don't want to hear it like, "Oh you'll be all right, he is in a better place now."

I don't want him to be in a better frickin' place, I want him to be right here with me.

These people barely knew Kev, what would they know? And then there's other shit people say about suicide like, "Suicide is such a cowardly thing to do. What about the people they leave behind? So selfish."

Really? If you are at the point where you're prepared to end your life by throwing yourself in front of a moving train, I'm sure you're neither a coward nor selfish – try staring at a moving train coming at *your* face.

I think it's more that you're stuck in your own head or in so much emotional pain you don't give a shit about others, you just want it all to stop. I have been right at that point, on the edge, staring death in the face, and all I was thinking, feeling and wanting was for the pain to stop. However, at the last second, for some reason, maybe I'm a coward, I stepped back.

At Mum's house, I'm sitting in the backyard and yes, the sun is shining and birds are singing and the funny old church ladies are fussing over the food that they had prepared earlier. Got to love the old church ladies, damn they made some nice cakes. I think the idea was to celebrate Kev's life, with a wake in the backyard with fancy cakes, finger food, champagne, beer and other crap. Honestly I just wanted to eat those cakes, drink that champagne, have a smoke and run away.

However, people just wanted to talk and talk and talk to me. It felt like they were talking at me. I had no idea about half of what they were saying nor did I give a shit, I just wanted this "funeral process" to stop and for my little brother to be back. This went on and on and on for a few hours. I finally left and drove home to have some time out and just, well… I guess, suffer by myself.

Days later it was my responsibility to pack up Kev's apartment and try and work out what the hell to do with his stuff. There were two reasons for this. Firstly, let's just say my family were a little too busy: my older brother lived a long way away, my sister was seven months' pregnant and mum was doing her cancer thing. Secondly, I was very close to Kev. I knew he would have hated others going through his personal belongings and I wanted to be respectful of his things and pack up his worldly life with a sense of dignity. Which brings me to what I was to witness next.

My older brother and mother had never bothered to visit Kev at his apartment. He had been there for two or three months and other than me, only my sister had visited a few times to drop stuff off and help him out. Nevertheless, they wanted to visit Kev's apartment now, after he was dead. I was fairly pissed off to start with. I thought... *why didn't they bother to visit him when he was alive?* I never asked though.

Kev and I had spent time fixing up his apartment and doing a "renovation rescue" one weekend, with my sister giving him some furniture, and honestly, the apartment looked great. He was seventeen years old and had a very cool apartment, a job, and he was so proud of himself. I was damn proud of him too; he had worked hard.

So, I met my mum, brother and sister at the apartment one morning and was feeling a little uneasy, knowing what Kev had been like with his personal stuff. I was still pissed off as I stood in front of Kev's apartment, I stepped forward to place the key in the lock and I stopped.

This is so wrong. I should be knocking on the door and Kev should be answering like last time I was here – which was only a week or so ago.

With my legs shaking and my stomach churning with anxiety, I turned the key and pushed the door open. The stale smell of a teenager's room wafted out as my family pushed past me and into Kev's apartment. From my perspective, they were only focused on what was inside. Their actions spoke volumes.

I was still standing in the doorway at this stage in a total stupor, then I witnessed the weirdest thing. My older brother and mother started going through every drawer, cupboard and cabinet like robots: open, look, take something, close, open cupboard, look, take something, close, open cabinet, look, take something and close.

I'm witnessing a robbery in Kev's apartment, carried out by his own family, and I was the one who let them in. I just wanted to vomit. Honestly I had not at that point accepted he was dead, I was kind of waiting for him to turn up at the apartment. I felt that I had betrayed him, I wanted to curl up and die right in the middle of the doorway.

In the next few weeks I managed to pack up Kev's life into boxes or garbage bags. I donated some of his belongings and carefully distributed the rest to family and friends. It was surprising hard to go through his personal stuff and decide what's important and what's not; what to keep and why does he have this or that? While I was doing all this, I was trying to get back to a "normal" life, returning back to the corporate world and to the regular bullshit. But I was suffering and not dealing with anything or anyone properly at that point.

ЖЖЖ

LESSONS LEARNT # 2:

*"Suicide is the inability to deal with one's current emotions, thoughts or situation.
It's a means of stopping the relentless pain, regardless of the outcome.*

*Understanding this I have finally stopped blaming myself for not doing enough.
It didn't matter how much I did it would never have been enough.*

*The nature of the free human spirit and choice,
be that aware or not."*

CHAPTER 5

BACK TO CORPORATE LIFE.

My career was going ok apart from the political tug of war at the office. At the time I kind of loved the challenges that my career threw at me and the pressure to perform when needed, it gave me a buzz… an addiction I guess. The fast-paced life of making deals and earning the big bucks.

The money, to be honest was keeping me in it, and I worked my ass off for it so I could go travel when allowed and sustain my deluded lifestyle. It was a dangerous game of give and take, that clearly was fucking with my soul and this game was time limited.

However, it was a great distraction during the day, I focused on doing what I needed to, in the hope of keeping my thoughts and emotions busy knowing once at alone, I would have to face what had happened with Kev, the family and where to go and what do to next. In the back of my mind I had the repetitive thoughts of just run and keep running and running.

I had so many realizations about life, people and the world. Most people could be understanding, kind and sometimes giving – this gave me a little more hope in people and life after what had happened. However, this was about to change somewhat. If you lose someone very close to you or experience another type of terrible tragedy in your life, you only have a set time period to get over it. From what I had seen or learnt, you've got three to five weeks. That's it, then it's game on again, and you better harden the fuck up and get on with life. Actually, I didn't want to get on with life and I was screwed in the head more than ever – confused and basically on autopilot.

A new lesson to learn: I was not working within the correct grieving time frame; I was mistaken and this was the start of some rough and bitter times. I was trying so hard to get my life back on track, believing or wishing all was going well and people were still all very understanding and kind. I was totally deluded looking back now.

One morning at work I was dragged into a meeting with management. The conversation was flowing; all was good and then one of the managers piped up. Let's call him "Bald-Ego." Bald-Ego informed everyone there were a few minor issues concerning one of my accounts. Turns out it was all fine, no dramas, but he was getting increasingly worked up and then started directing his bullshit at me. He made it quite personal and then harpooned me with something about how he and others had had to cover for me while I was off work. *What the heck?* Such a 'deer in headlights' moment: *What the hell was he going on about?*

I stared Bald-Ego in the eyes for a moment. *You prick, you're referring to the time when my little brother killed himself.* That had been about five weeks earlier. I could feel my blood boiling; my face was getting extremely hot and I looked around the room and noticed the other managers preparing themselves to restrain me. They all looked a little shocked too from what had just been said. The thing is, generally whatever is going on in my head is written all over my face, so to speak. No poker faces here. All I wanted to do was stand up, walk over to him and smack him in the head with an office chair. Yes, I was developing some very unhealthy anger issues.

The fact was, I had taken an extra three days off work because I was already on holiday to start with – nothing more serious than that – and the unreasonable and total bullshit attack from Bald-Ego really pissed me off. I had given bloody, sweat and tears to this company and this was the attitude – or lack of basic human empathy and respect I got? *Seriously?*

Deep inside me, like someone flicking a switch, my attitude towards management and corporate life turned. At the time I had no idea but this was something of a defining moment. Something began to change inside that would set the pace for the coming years, with some surprising twists thrown in.

As I walked out of the meeting, my blood was still boiling. *What the fuck am I doing in corporate land?* I kept asking myself. I did love some parts of it but it seemed to be eating me alive dealing with people and situations like that. Yet the money was good and gave me the freedom to do other things when I was not working – which was pretty much never.

Realization number *"two hundred and bloody forty-eight"* for 2007: I was trapped in a vicious circle. This situation would repeat itself many more times again until I got the message to move on and change my career and ultimately my life.

But on that particular day I decided to run. It was only a little run, and not too far away. I was too full of fear to leave corporate land at this point and paranoid as hell that no one else would employ me. I was very down on myself and had lost a lot of faith and confidence in the world around me.

I decided to plan a trip to somewhere for four weeks or so, and get the hell out of my current life and work situation. I needed space and travel seemed to be the answer. Travel always made my life more fun, interesting and cleared my head. That was just what I needed, some travelling. *Where will I go?* I thought.

ЖЖЖ

CHAPTER 6:
TIME TO RUN.

The thought of Africa excited me: nature, new cultures and the wildlife. Back when I was eighteen, I had seen a movie about the mountain gorillas called *Gorillas in the Mist* and it had totally inspired me. It told the incredible story of Dian Fossey and how she lived in the mountains of Rwanda where she studied and cared for many of the mountain gorillas before she was unfortunately killed.

Thinking back to the time when I watched the movie, I remembered promising myself that one day I would visit the great mountain gorillas of Rwanda. I would come face to face with a silverback and sit with the gorillas in their own natural environment with no fences, no walls – just they and I together. *What an amazing thing to do*, I thought to myself.

The trip I booked was an overland "adventure" tour (and when they said adventure, they *meant* adventure) to cover Kenya, Uganda, and Tanzania and to visit the mountain gorillas in… Well, at the time I just assumed Rwanda. *How little did I know…?* Another one of those moments when an assumption would lead to one of the most frightening times of my life.

So, my trip was booked and I was so damn excited about travelling again. I managed to get three nights in Dubai on the way back to visit some friends and chill out before returning to crazy corporate land. *What a great way to ease my mind and escape from my past, the death of my brother and the corporate bullshit life in which I chose to live in,* I thought.

A few weeks before I was leaving for my African adventure, some colleagues questioned me on why the hell I was going to Africa. They pointed out that my travel history was splattered with near-death experiences and the picking up of unheard illnesses. My response was to laugh it off.

I will be fine, no worries, all will be good – and for God's sake, I think I have had my share of bad luck or misfortune; the bucket of bad luck has to be empty by now...

...

I began to recall my backpacking trip through Vietnam and Cambodia a few years earlier when I had come very close to losing my life – or so I had thought at the time. Leading up to my trip I had a few instances of self-diagnosed food poisoning. Clearly I was not a doctor and had never bothered to see one either – which was going to come back to bite me hard on the ass.

Picture this: a beautiful, peaceful, tropical oasis; an island with white sandy beaches and little private bamboo cabins dotted along the seashore, complete with lush green vegetation and tall, swaying palm trees. I was very fortunate to have one of the best little bamboo cabins on the island. I could even see the white sandy beach from my front door. I was truly in heaven. Oh, the bliss, the beauty, the tranquility! *Could it get any better than this?*

Well… no!

Late one night I awoke in a total flat-spin; my body was trying to kill itself from the inside out. The pain was unbearable, my stomach was beating the shit out of itself, and it felt like someone was kicking the hell out of my kidneys. I was saturated with sweat, I was shaking and, wait for it… seized with uncontrollable gut-wrenching vomiting. Then, much to my horror, my ass exploded! *What the hell is going on,* was all I could think.

Was I going to die? Bring it on, I thought, with the way I felt right then… *Just kill me now.*

This went on for hours. In the meantime, I managed to get some help. Well, not exactly help: basically someone to stand there and watch me vomit on myself while my ass continued to explode randomly. Remember I was on an island: an oasis of bliss and calm. Turns out it didn't come with medical staff, just people to stand around and watch you suffer in your own vomit and shit.

After about five hours of this going on, it just stopped. Just like that. No more pain, no more vomiting and no more exploding ass… Nothing at all. *It must have been food poisoning again, great.* Then I could get back to relaxing and enjoying this beautiful place. It was an island (which I renamed Vomit Island) just off the coast of Vietnam. And what a country!

A week later we finally made it to Cambodia, somewhere I had so wanted to visit for years – a top five on my bucket list.

Still feeling a little weak from the Vomit Island experience but in one piece, life was great again. Wandering around Phnom Penh and taking in the sights, I realized what an amazing place it was. At dinner, I began to get very excited about our plans to visit some of the museums, other culturally important sights and of course the Killing Fields (not exactly excited about that, more interested) the following day. Again… *How little did I know?* That night pretty much changed my life – or at least the way I viewed life for the short term anyway.

Suddenly, just like on Vomit Island, the same things starting happening again… *Holy shit!* But this time tenfold and super intense; I was going in and out of consciousness and my room-mate found me on the bathroom floor. At that point he leaned down to see if I was ok and I remember looking at him, his eyes staring back at me, with a face full of worry and total doom. This freaked me out and I knew this time I was in deep shit. Next thing I knew I was being rushed to a hospital and I found myself laying again on a bathroom floor.

Where the hell am I and what is going on?

The pain at this point was fingernail pullingly intense, I was covered in sweat from head to toe, but still freezing, and the waves of pain were making me black out. Oh, and the vomiting!

I felt like I was vomiting up my shoe along with a large feral animal. As time went on I was blacking out more and more; the pain throughout my body was so intense that I thought I should just smash my head on the toilet and knock myself out. I started thinking I was about to die, and these thoughts became stronger and stronger, racing around in my head again and again.

Tim, you're dying, Tim, you're dying, Tim, this is it, this is where you die. No fucking way… I'm not dying in a pool of vomit.

But half-lying and half-leaning against the toilet bowl, I just thought *to hell with it*. It was all too intense and I let go of any hope. Laid out on the toilet floor with my head resting on my arm, I accepted it was all over, death was coming, and there was nothing I could do.

The sensation of being very light and calm came over me, I was now completely detached from all pain and reality, just like they depict in the Hollywood movies. In all honesty my life – my whole entire life – flashed before my eyes and it was amazing and beautiful: an incredible journey. All the good times and all the people that I had held so dear to me and loved, each of their faces flashed one by one right in front of my eyes. The bliss I felt! So much peace and the sense of being in close company with the divine.

I was dying and it felt great. At least so I thought…

What I experienced that day, those sensations within my body and mind will stay with me for the rest of my life. It was better than any drug I had ever taken. It was pure and it was divine peace.

Waking up in a bed with things hanging out of my arm and wrist, I was so high – totally off my head. I felt amazing and as I was trying to work out where I was (which was in a small clinic in the back streets of Phnom Penh).

WOW, life is good, I feel amazing. I'm alive!

A travel companion appeared in front of me and asked if I was ok.

I was like, "Oh yeah this is amazing, you should try some of this," pointing at the tube in my arm. I started laughing and asked her to please take a photo of me. Ok, I was on holiday, travelling and I guess at the time it was pretty funny; I was drugged-up to my eyeballs with not a care in the world.

The doctor came in about ten minutes later and spoke with me in an interesting, yet understandable, broken English, "We have plane ready for you, you very sick, we fly you to Bangkok to operate, you agree?"

Hmm… Cool, a plane ride that sounds fun… Oh what the heck? Did he just say operation? No way am I having an operation. I remembered I was booked to go to the Killing Fields the next day at six a.m.

The doctor went on to say my gall bladder was severely infected and something to do with it being six times larger than normal. *And that means what? I'm sure I can take some drugs and wait till I get back home to have an operation.*

At that point I told the doctor I was fine, and that there was no need to operate and fly me to Bangkok; I assured him all would be ok. The doctor totally disagreed and insisted on me getting on the plane and he left the room to go and do some paperwork.

Somehow I managed to check myself out of the clinic and get a taxi back to the hotel, with the only single thought of *I have come this far and I don't want to miss out on the Killing fields.* Stupid? Yes, but I had lived to fight another day.

I got to see the Killing Fields, arriving back home a week later for some emergency surgery. After the surgery, my doctor paid me a visit and added, "What the hell where you thinking? You could have died from this. You're one lucky guy to get away with that."

So, with that in mind – and I had had a few other trips in the past that had gone in a similar way – I guess the work colleagues were onto something and I knew I should have been a better listener. However, Africa was calling. I was itching to get on that plane and get away from my past and my corporate career. All I could think was, *give me some nature, wildlife and fun and all will be great.* Happy days. Or so I thought…

ЖЖЖ

LESSON LEARNT: #3

"In the midst of dying or at least the sensation of thinking I was, was the most empowering and invigorating experience of my life.

To let go of all, I mean everything, dreams, career, family and life itself, opened up a realm of tranquility beyond words.

Letting go, rather than fighting, in life sometimes, can be the cure to great suffering."

CHAPTER 7:
AFRICA, HERE I COME…

Finally, the big day was almost upon me and soon I would be off to Africa. At the same time, I learnt that my roommate had decided he was moving out. *Bloody hell, more drama.* I thought. *And I was just starting to get back on my feet.*

He was going to move out while I would be in Africa. *Bad timing or what?* I had so been hoping to just escape from my life to Africa and have no worries for when I returned… Now I needed to find a new frickin' roommate.

This took the edge off my excitement. I just needed to suck it up and focus on running away and enjoying Africa. The roommate drama would sort itself out later, I decided.

So, I was at the airport and all checked in. I was feeling ok about my new adventure. This was going to be one amazing trip, I told myself. Suddenly, a smack in the face from the past… The last time I was at the airport standing right where I was, the family and I were all taking dumb-ass photos of each other. We were all laughing and having fun. Kev was alive and we were about to spend two weeks in Thailand. The memories of that holiday and of Kev brought up so many mixed emotions.

I was still not getting my head around Kev's suicide. The more I ran, the more it chased me down and tormented me like some sort of sick torture. I guessed one day I would have to sit down with myself and stare it in the face and just deal with it, but at that moment, I was running away to Africa. Disappearing seemed like the perfect plan.

Feeling all over the place emotionally with my roommate moving out, memories of my little brother's suicide and the excitement of my trip to Africa, I boarded the plane for a fourteen-hour flight to Dubai, then another flight to Nairobi, Kenya. My stomach was full of butterflies just thinking about what I was going to experience and see, and my expectations were high.

Ok, that was the first mistake of the trip and there were many more to come. Setting realistic expectations was not my thing.

Long flight: *sleeping pills or no sleeping pills*; I asked myself. *Fourteen hours on a plane? Hmmm... Fuck it. I shall take some sleeping pills.* Checked the packet; quick read of the instructions (take one to one and a half). Ok cool. Popped one and waited for about an hour. NOTHING. I had a glass of wine. Still nothing... Wide-awake. *Noooooo. These pills are crap.* Another hour passed and I was still wide-awake. Ok, I popped another pill and ten minutes later: *hoooo eeee... damn. I'm feeling sleepy.* That was the last thing I was to remember.

Next thing I knew, I had some person leaning other me shaking me, "Wake up sir. Sir, sir, wake up." It was the airhostess and we were about to land in Dubai.

Turns out I had read the instructions wrong. It was take a half to one pill and I had taken two and I had no idea where I was, who I was, or that the plane was about to land in some country – by then I couldn't even recall where I was going. Before I knew it, I was wandering around the Dubai airport trying to think what I needed to do next and wondering how the hell I got there.

After some time, I managed to work out that I had a connecting flight to Nairobi which was departing in the next three hours and I needed to get my shit together. I also needed a shower and I needed one right away to sober me up.

Where the hell do you find a shower in an unknown airport?

Stumbling around the airport I finally found some signs to a sports club of all things and YES they had showers… *Brilliant!*

All cleaned up and only a little sobered up I boarded the plane bound for Nairobi. Finally, it was all happening, I would be in Africa in fewer than six hours: in a new country, with new cultures, meeting new people, and just the thought of seeing the mountain gorillas brought a tear to my eye. Yes, I know I was still whacked out on pills and a little unstable emotionally.

Ж Ж Ж

CHAPTER 8:
WELCOME TO AFRICA AND ENJOY YOUR TOUR.

L anding in the Nairobi airport, I had no idea what to expect. *Best to expect the worst then I can work forward from there,* I thought. And it was a good thing I did. I found my backpack, got through immigration and then stumbled out into the arrivals hall to a welcoming team of what seemed to be half of Kenya. Somewhat intense! The smells and sights of a new country's airport arrivals hall. What more could you ask for?

It was overwhelmingly obvious at the time that I was the only Westerner, white person, non-local (not sure what the politically correct term is) that I could see. Straight up, I felt like a target and was paralyzed with paranoia. Remember I suffer with depression and anxiety, which comes from being a little fearsome at times and I get thinking and *bam*, uncontrollable thoughts appear. And this time, it was paranoia. I slowly made my way through the sea of people to meet some local guy that was going to take me to my hotel somewhere in Nairobi.

The local guy, a very nice man, informed me it was five thirty p.m. and that was "crazy time" in the great city of Nairobi, so I should sit back and relax because the ride was going to be a long one. And long it was.

Crazy time in Nairobi consisted of bumper-to-bumper traffic – or that should read bumper touching bumper – with thousands and thousands of people running around everywhere, all on a mission to get somewhere. It was like an uncontrollable riot with no actual violence, all my senses were being assaulted repeatedly, and my heart was racing while my eyes were forced wide opened. I was alive. I was feeling, seeing, smelling and living. I was in Africa, damn it, and it was so in-my-face.

The sleeping pills had long worn off; I knew where I was and that was somewhere that was going to wake me up beyond all my mismanaged expectations.

After several hours of weaving our way across town, we arrived at the hotel. *Hmmm…* It actually looked more like a prison camp – a nice prison camp, mind you. The whole place was fenced and gated with security guards everywhere, equipped to take down a small rebel regime. I came to understand this more, further down the track on my adventures in Africa.

Safely within the hotel grounds, I checked in and was off to my room to relax for a bit. Later that night it was time to meet the local guide, get the run-down of the trip and meet my fellow travelers with whom I would be spending the next four weeks. All I wished for was a chilled and fun group of people to travel with – no stress, no dramas.

After the meeting had finished I sat outside on one of the hotel's porches by myself to have a drink. Soaking up the Nairobi night air I reflected on the past day or so: my flight and the sleeping pill issue, the trip from the airport to the hotel, and all the crazy shit I had seen of this new culture as I stared out of the small taxi's window – the people, the noise and the different aromas. I had an uneasy feeling that there was a bit of unrest or tension in the air, the feeling just before all turns to shit. I just put it down to my paranoia.

...

Maybe it wasn't without good reason. The last time I had had that feeling was back in the late 1990's on my way to Egypt with a friend, where we planned to meet my sister. I had got in a night earlier than her so I could try and see more of Cairo – what an amazing place. I had sensed the feeling that something bad was going to happen – I thought of an earthquake happening, which seemed totally unreasonable. An earthquake in Cairo? Clearly I needed to up my medication.

We had arrived in the capital in the late evening and then were at the hotel by about 1.30 a.m. Several hours later the hotel caught fire and I was extremely lucky to get out in one piece. Not a good wake-up call: people trying to bash down your door at 5 a.m. to recommend you that you need to get out and get out now! The best part about this was that the fire was in the stairwell (the only way out) and there was no power – so no lights – just total darkness. The smell of smoke and the sounds of glass smashing and people screaming made the hairs on the back of my neck stand straight up. I had the feeling in my stomach of… *this may be the end.*

Two local guys helped my friend and me to communicate with the emergency services and somehow we managed to run, or literally hover, down the stairwell like some cartoon characters, through the flames, sliding out into the lobby, which was half a foot deep in water, then onto the street and to safety. Note to self: best to stay home and watch the Discovery channel in future.

…

Realizing that I was literally thousands of miles from following my own advice, I thought about the place in which I now found myself. Kenya, where, at the time, I clearly had no idea what the state of play was politically. It was mid-2007, right at the start of the Mungiki sect uprising, and the Kenyan government was trying to control the situation.

I did not see any direct effects of it, however, only the news and local people freaking out, advising us not to go here or there. We were to have several days of unknowns and basically shitting ourselves on what might happen as we travelled overland throughout Kenya, around the areas of conflict while returning back to Nairobi.

Putting political conflict aside for a moment, I met the group. They all seemed to be fairly cool people at first sight but it was about to change once we all got on the truck and on our way.

First stop: The Maasai Mara. Damn long drive, I have to say, especially when you have four total red-neck 'missing-link' types from Australia who think it's really cool to get blind drunk and harass the hell out of the other people, be that passengers or local people... *Go figure men?* And this shit went on for... well until they got off the truck.

I'm not sure why you would want to travel around Africa completely paralytic 24/7 and miss out on so much amazing culture, scenery and wildlife but from what I could see, apparently it was a cool and hip thing to do if you were Australian. Get paralytic and travel around the world. Clearly I missed that memo.

Aside from the "Aussie paralytic team", I was having major issues with my malaria medication. I was tripping out hard, hallucinating, and massively paranoid and having the most screwed up dreams you could imagine. Yet it did seem to make things more interesting.

The first night in the Maasai Mara, we were in the middle of nowhere with bush everywhere and freaky sounding animals in the distance. A bunch of Westerners with all our Western crap, sitting around a campfire, when one of the local guides informs us all (as I was just about to pick up my torch and head to my tent) of some quite disturbing news… "A small child has just been killed by a wild buffalo that has been wandering around the area, it's not the first time this has happened and the locals are off to kill it." Great news, just what I wanted to hear as I walked in the dark to my tent. I felt so sorry too for the poor little kid and the family, what a horrific thing to happen. Life was tough in the Maasai Mara.

In my tent and not feeling very safe at all with just some thin material protecting me from the wildness of Africa, the malaria medication had kicked in again and my paranormally paranoid mind was rampantly out of control. *Will the crazy wild buffalo get into the campsite and into my tent and maul me to death while I sleep? And what about the Aussie paralytic team, what the hell are they doing?* I could hear them in the background with their obnoxious, drunken, hyena-laughter. It was becoming increasingly obvious to the other travelers that this was a problem for all involved. *Maybe the crazed buffalo will eat them?*

The next morning, we were off to see the sights of the great Maasai Mara – what an eye opener to see how other people exist, living off the land. And how basic life was out there: no TVs, no AC, no computers and *excellent*, no emails! They seemed to not have much at all, not like us Westerners. They just had their little huts, some livestock, their smiling faces and the people in their community. They all seemed relatively happy and content.

We did the normal tourist thing with the now very hung-over Aussie paralytic team in tow, and visited an arts and crafts village. *What the hell are we going to see?* I was thinking on the way out there. *There is not much stuff around to get all arts and crafty here.* But what an amazing place! Much to my surprise, although these people had very little, damn, they made stuff out of anything, and it was so creative and beautiful. Warrior masks, bracelets, necklaces, weapons – the list of astonishing stuff went on. It was very inspiring.

Next stop: a very, very basic school with a few Westerners running around helping out the locals, I guess on a volunteer program. *Good on them,* I thought. However, they seemed to have a small hint of arrogance towards our group, along the lines of a "look at me, I am saving the world and what are you doing about it?" type of attitude. Not too sure what that was all about, but it was great seeing them working hard to make a difference. I feel a little uncomfortable about the whole charity work thing. Travelling around and seeing some developing countries, the local people have pretty much been doing the same thing for hundreds of years and life goes on. They all seemed happy and not grabbing at their iPhones every two seconds to update their Facebook status with "checked in - #very hot #school visit – Maasai Mara" as we do in the west

I have always been interested in doing charity work. You know, 'save the world' kind of stuff, but after witnessing what we Western people generally deem to be important, that is mostly commercial stuff and status. Stuff that we can wear and play with, or show to others saying, "Look at me, look at this latest blah-blah thing, I am so complete and feel great, I now fit in."

Then in five minutes the new updated blah-blah thing appears and it's like, "Oh no I am not worthy anymore until I have that new updated blah-blah thing." Scary how the world works in the West. Even scarier that I was so damn personally entrenched in it and in no position to force my standard of living on anyone.

The people of the Maasai Mara were amazing to me: such genuine, beautiful people – people with not much in material terms but nonetheless so welcoming and kind. That experience made me feel pathetic, I had so much and I was still miserable with my situation – and a little ungrateful too.

We did a few safaris and loads of game-watching in the national park. It was overwhelming to experience so much space – as far as the eye could see – and so many different animals, some of which I had only ever seen in a zoo. It was awe-inspiring to witness so many animals in their natural environment.

The Maasai Mara adventure was speedily coming to an end and the next day we travelled overland back to Nairobi for two nights before starting our new adventure: more of Kenya, then Uganda, and the mountain gorillas. The great news is that most of the Aussie paralytic team were disembarking in Nairobi to go wreak havoc on other countries and cultures. I was so happy to see the back of them, and I realized we were picking up ten more people in Nairobi for our next African adventure. *What would this bring to the truck dynamics?*

On the journey back, I started to notice the local guide and the truck driver becoming increasingly uptight and disturbed. Chatting with them at one of the stops, I discovered they had received news that the "shit had hit the fan" with the Mungiki sect, a violent group that controlled vast slum areas in Nairobi and that were becoming increasingly politicized. It had commenced a campaign of horrific violence in certain areas around the capital which, from all reports, we were driving straight into.

This is the time when you sit back, try to relax, and do some breathing exercises. Staring out the window of the truck, seeing local people getting their stuff sorted to move quickly, the general feel of unrest was all very concerning. But then realizing I was in a foreign country, didn't speak Swahili, and I was travelling in a large green truck-cum-bus-thing that was full of white people. *We're SCREWED!* Was all I could think. We were such a target, *for sure, without a doubt,* and I was still struggling with my mind-altering malaria medication… Paranoid much? *HELL YEAH!*

I spoke further with the driver and the guide. These guys were local men and had seen it all before, which was very sad because they were such beautiful people and no one wants to experience that shit. Nervously they assured us all that they had found a way to go around the trouble areas and kind of "sneak" into Nairobi and all would be fine.

Looking at them, expressions of worry were just dripping off their faces. *How the fuck do you sneak a large, green truck-bus thing, full of white people into Nairobi?* In the end they did an amazing job to get us all safely back to Nairobi and into the hotel. All was fine, well fine for us anyway, as we were in the hotel's secured compound, which I was finally beginning to appreciate. For the others, it was chaos: the killing and burning alive of many Kenyans was truly a sad state of affairs.

I managed to meet many local people in Kenya, and they were such authentic, kind and loving people that my heart went out to them. I just wished, and wished hard, that their country would find peace soon. So, easy to sit in your big old comfortable chair watching CNN news as it reports on atrocities like these and think, *Oh it's just on TV.*

To see this amazing country and its culture, to hear about its history and more importantly, to have the opportunity to talk with the local people and be touched by their stories and touched by their lives was a blessing. And it was also very humbling. Now every time I see stories in the news about Kenya or Africa in general, I have a totally different outlook. Thank you, Kenya.

...

By about a week later we had covered thousands of kilometers and had seen some amazing sights across Kenya and Uganda. The ten new travelling companions were all settling in and were good people – fun and drama-free – and the Aussie paralytic team was a distant memory, along with my pathetic existence back home.

What a great way to spend my time travelling around Africa! No mobile phones, no emails and no corporate bullshit. The only real stress was trying to put my tent up late at night without harpooning myself in the face with one of the tent poles.

The place was spectacular and I was enjoying everything that Africa had to offer – there were so many things. And to think, you could sit on the side of the road in Uganda eating a sandwich and look across and see fields of tea plantations that stretched to the horizon. Tea in Africa had never even crossed my mind. Every day was like that; being in Africa was like being in a relationship. The more time you spent with her, the more she reveals, and as you got to learn, you came to hate and love so many different things about her. But beware, she bites. And she was about to dig her teeth into me and bite hard.

We made our way out towards the borders of Rwanda and the Democratic Republic of the Congo, through picturesque, lush green valleys, then slowly upwards high into the mountains along thin and badly maintained dirt roads. These roads (loosely speaking; they were more like little dirt tracks) had taken many lives in the past and as we edged along the thin, dirt track high up in the mountains, I leant out the truck window to take in the awe-inspiring landscape that went on and on for hundreds of kilometers.

In the distance I could make out forms of what looked like volcanoes. The place looked like something out of Jurassic Park, it was one of the most majestic landscapes I had ever seen. People say some places in the world are breathtaking, well this place took my breath *and* stopped my heart, particularly cause while leaning out the window I looked directly downwards and could see the truck's wheels right on the edge of the dirt track. There was about an inch and then it was a sheer drop off – straight down a valley about five hundred meters deep. Moments like those can only make you forget about the past and give you the feeling of being totally alive and present.

Heading back down the mountains of Uganda into one of the many valleys, we made it to a quaint, little village. It was as though it had stopped in time: back in the nineteen hundreds. One long dirt track represented the main street, with a few old, wooden and brick buildings either side, all in need of repair. Looking around you could feel you were deep inside Africa and from what I could see, there were no other tourists but us, all packed into the large green truck. This was the place to set up camp for a few days, take it easy, wander around the village and hang out with some locals if possible.

More importantly, this was the place I had been waiting for. In the next few days we would set off from here to see the mountain gorillas in Uganda or neighboring Rwanda. Well… that was my thinking, and again, *how little did I know.* Never expect anything except the unexpected in Africa. What was about to unfold in the coming days was going to challenge me to the very core and show me what I was capable of in extreme circumstances…

ЖЖЖ

WELCOME TO THE DRC!

L ate in the afternoon while sitting around chatting with some of the guys with whom I was travelling, I recalled my teenage dream. *Damn…* I thought. *I am going to see the mountain gorillas in the next few days.* The excitement was pumping through every cell of my body and I could not have been happier. My expectations were high.

This dream, however, would turn out to be more like one of those super-surreal nightmares where you are not sure when you wake up if it actually happened or not, and it takes you about ten minutes to come to your senses and realize everything is ok.

The next morning, we all met with our guide from the truck and some funny little local guy turned up too. He was full of attitude (short man thing maybe?) and carrying a little leather briefcase. To add to all of this, he had on the longest pair of socks I had ever seen in my life. They were pulled up almost over his knees. Looking closer he had his pants tucked into his incredibly long socks too. Total classic! Turns out later the long socks were more than just a fashion statement.

This funny little local guy got up and started talking about our imminent trek and how things would work, plus things that we needed to be aware of for our safety and that of the mountain gorillas. He was the official "go-to guy" on the subject of gorillas in these parts: the "Gorilla Agent", as I dubbed him. It was his show, on his terms and God forbid you cross him.

He went on to explain, "When we are entering the Democratic Republic of the Congo (DRC) be sure to…" I stopped suddenly.

What the heck…? Did he just say the DRC? He added that we would have full military protection from the Ugandan border to the National Park's base camp where we would start our trek. Every single self-preserving alarm bell in my head went off! *I don't want to go to the frickin' DRC,* I thought. *I want to go to Rwanda; I want to be just like Dian Fossey in the movie Gorillas in the Mist.* There was no fucking way I was going into the DRC.

With my internal alarm bells ringing loudly, I thought of a recent documentary that I had watched on the DRC guerrillas. Those were the other kind of gorillas with the big machine guns and machetes. These guys were brutally killing people for fun and were basically tearing the country apart using the mountain gorillas and locals as some kind of sick bargaining tool, so the documentary said.

The deal was that the guerrillas would threaten to slaughter the mountain gorillas, local people and anyone in their way if the government and the international community did not agree to their terms. That was my very limited understanding of the current situation in the DRC in mid-2007, anyway.

So, what the Gorilla Agent was saying was that we were about to go trekking "for fun" in the neighborhood of the guerrillas with guns. And this was on a holiday that I had chosen to take to try and distance myself from my little brother's suicide and my time-limited career. Instead I was walking straight into another unbelievably and truly screwed up situation. What the hell was I doing?

The meeting continued. Gorilla Agent gave very strict instructions for what all trekkers should take with them, which was the bare minimum of one liter of water for every two to three hours of trekking and in his own style, long socks for the entire trek too. Then, depending on our level of physical fitness and trekking abilities, we were broken up into groups of five to seven people per group. I choose the super easy trekking group. I had broken my back when I was eighteen (but that's another story!) and from time to time I had a few problems on long treks with my left leg not working properly, so I thought I would play it safe.

The super easy trek I chose was to be around five hours in total: into the jungle, up the mountain, view the mountain gorillas and then back to base camp. It all sounded so easy and fun. *What an amazing adventure we all were about to experience,* I thought. I was overwhelmed with the desire to just get going and see the beautiful creatures.

.....

The big day arrived; it was show time. Up at four am, showered, with trekking gear on, I realized I had forgotten to pack long socks and only had very short ones. I reassured myself that this would be fine. I packed three liters of water and a small amount of food for my five-hour trek and at the last minute I threw a handful of those hard sugar candies into my pack, always great for a boost of energy.

I was raring to go and so excited to be able to finally be on the verge of fulfilling one of my (literally) wildest dreams of coming face to face with the mountain gorillas and in particular – fingers crossed – a silver back. Thinking about the day ahead, I felt nervous in the way that you are on a first date, not truly knowing how it will all go, yet filled with excitement and hoping your expectations will be met.

We drove for about thirty to forty minutes from the campsite and got to the border around five a.m. By this time the sun was just starting to rise, shining a little light on a new day, a new adventure and a day that would offer me an insight into how far I could be physically, mentally and emotionally pushed.

I jumped out of the truck and pretty much bounced over to what I thought was the border crossing point. I was surprised to discover that we in fact seemed to be on someone's farm. There was thick bush land all about us, a field to the left and a very old thatched wooden fence in front of me with a dirt road that disappeared off into the wilderness. The road was blocked by an old, rusty steel pole lying across it. I noticed a large sign saying, "You are now leaving Uganda and entering Zaire." (Zaire being the former colonial name of the DRC, discarded in the late 1990's.) That was the extent of the border security. No x-ray machines, no security guards or lengthy queues, just a rusty, old steel pole to step over. *Brilliant, this is too easy,* I thought…

Gorilla Agent was in tow and stopped us all for a moment to reiterate that he was the man in charge and we should do everything he said. He followed up with further instructions not to take any photos of the border crossing or the military personnel. Apparently the military guys were a little camera shy and were prone to shoot you if you photographed the border crossing. I couldn't see any military men, so I took a quick snapshot of the crossing anyway.

Like a group of very excited school kids on a sugar high, we took off. Jumping over the rusty, old pipe and into no man's land (literally, as it was a strip of land about five hundred meters between the two borders) we chatted away with such high expectations of seeing the great mountain gorillas and spending time with them. We were then met by another old thatched wooden fence, this time with barbed wire on top of it. There was a small gateway with an old truck tire leaning against it. This was the official gateway to the great DRC.

Staring at the big, old truck tire, I was still a bit perplexed as to the lack of security or anything that even resembled a border crossing. Turning my attention to what was beyond and slowly mouthing the words… "Oh…. my… God!" my body started to shake uncontrollably. We were about to enter something like the movie set of "Blood Diamond" and I was shitting myself. It was a village of sorts, essentially eight to ten rundown buildings with a dirt road through the middle. Military personnel were everywhere – these guys were the definition of "Big Scary Mother Fuckers" so to speak, or BSMF. They were scarier than scary. Six to seven feet tall, built like super-human warriors, they all carried large machine guns and looked like they could pick you up, snap you in half and eat you for lunch. I just hoped they were not hungry.

The Gorilla Agent pushed past me and rolled the truck tire back, allowing us all to walk into the DRC. We were herded like cattle towards a building that was the immigration processing office. Handing over our passports we sat to wait for our visas to be completed and were told not to move. *Nervous, much?*

The place was incredibly intense; it made Nairobi's 'crazy o'clock' look like a beautiful English flower show in the spring. Nothing, and I mean *nothing* I had ever seen before in my travels came close to this. The poverty here was ubiquitous and the energy in the air was one of overwhelming fear and mistrust. *Or was that just me being super paranoid?*

Sitting there observing my new surroundings, I tried to get my head around what I was seeing. This place seemed to be off the development scale, never mind third world, this was fifth world at best. As we waited, more and more people and military guys started turning up, some by foot or on those funky homemade wooden bikes, and in extremely old beaten up Bongo vans. The military guys were also all geared up with machine guns, in addition to handguns, machetes and hand grenades strapped to them like some sort of life jackets. One of the BSMFs was casually leaning up against a building smoking, with a rocket launcher hanging off his shoulder, complete with rocket attached and ready to go. You don't see that every day! I was getting more and more uncomfortable with my new environment by the minute.

After a short wait our visas were approved and we are all ready to leave "scary town" and go trekking in the mountainous jungles of the DRC – and incidentally the home turf of the guerrillas with big guns – for fun!

I had never before experienced the emotions I was feeling. Total bone-shaking excitement at the prospect of fulfilling my teenage dream and seeing the magnificent mountain gorillas in their own habitat, combined with the overpowering fear and anxiety of being shot in the face or chopped up into little pieces or even kidnapped. Talk about a battle of the minds and emotions.

Each group was allotted its transport to the National Park's base camp – essentially 1970's Bongo vans – and ours came complete with rusted-out floor, doors and roof, and every square millimeter had a dent in it. Clearly windows were optional too: three of six windows still intact were apparently fairly good. *No five-star luxury for me today then,* I mused. Each Bongo van was supplied with three local military guys. Yes! Those BSMFs. *Brilliant…* We would get to sit right next to them in a tiny, beaten up Bongo van for an hour.

All aboard, we were off; a convoy of four beaten-up little Bongo vans packed with some very white Westerners. I was jammed in the middle of one of the vans and had a BSMF military man pretty much sitting on my face. With no room to move an inch for an hour, and with the barrel of his machine gun repeatedly hitting me on the side of the head at every bump, I wondered if it could get any better than this…

Driving through the many villages on the way to the base camp was an extraordinary and sobering experience. Looking out the cracked front windscreen of the Bongo van I was feeling so alive and in awe of my new surroundings. The place was epic. Village life in the DRC looked astonishingly primitive. No electricity, no running water and houses that were beyond basic – and to think I had been whining about taking a cold shower. This was truly survival of the fittest.

Life there was unbelievably simple compared to mine back home with all its countless luxuries. The poverty was completely in-your-face, this was a hard existence by anyone's standards and to top it off, the ongoing violent Kivu conflict was right on their doorsteps.

What made these people keep going?

In one of the villages, some of my travelling companions began waving, smiling and taking photos of the locals as the convoy drove slowly by. A handful of locals were smiling back and waving in bemusement, yet most seemed distinctly unimpressed.

Hearing what sounded like rocks bouncing off the sides of the van as more and more locals came out of their roadside huts, I realized that they were actually throwing rocks and sticks, and were spitting at us. We and our armed protectors were clearly not welcome. Although I was aware there were numerous possible reasons for this, I never fully understood why.

Finally, we made it to the base camp in one piece, although the side of my head was a little sore. The BSMF military men handed us over to the National Park guides and their armed security forces. These guys seemed a whole lot happier to see us.

Walking up to the National Park's base camp, which was at the top of a large, grassy verge, the landscape before me was spectacular, opening unto a massive valley that stretched for kilometers and was dotted with little farmhouses and fields of fresh green crops. It was like heaven on earth, the beauty of which was quite breathtaking and the mountains... *The mountains! Finally,* I was there to see for myself the home of the mountain gorillas, and unfortunately the guerrillas, and we were all about to experience it firsthand.

Meeting our guide for the trek, who came with two-armed security forces guys, we got a very basic brief on what to expect. It was hard to understand what the hell the guide was saying. His English was very basic. What I could understand was that it was going to be a relatively simple five-hour round trip with the odd bit of hard terrain and thick jungle to negotiate. He also added it was important to tuck our pants into our "long" socks due to the high numbers of ants. *Ants?* I thought to myself. *Surely ants can't be that bad.*

Sitting on the grassy verge, taking in the amazing sights of the incredible landscape, I noticed the other groups were all getting ready to go and each of them had five-armed security forces guys packing machine guns, hand guns and machetes. *Why do they have more armed security guys than us?* The question ran through my mind before I was distracted with the movement of my group leaving. I would return to that thought quite uncomfortably in the next few days.

ЖЖЖ

CHAPTER 10:
GORILLAS IN THE MIST... WHERE?

With excited anticipation, we started our five-hour trek into the great unknown to finally meet the mountain gorillas. It was about 6.30a.m. when we started out, the air was rather fresh and crisp, and the mountains ahead of us were still partly covered in a fine layer of early morning mist.

The group I was trekking with consisted of an Australian guy in his mid–twenties – a bit of a macho man, an English girl in her early twenties – a bookworm-type – and an American father/daughter combo consisting of – an old guy in his fifties and an eighteen or nineteen-year-old girl.

Trekking for over an hour before our first resting point – *holy shit* – the terrain was impossible. The first thirty minutes were fine, basically wandering through someone's cornfields, before we hit the great face of the DRC mountainous jungle. This was where the machetes came in handy and the security guys hacked a path for us feeble Westerners. We were virtually on our hands and knees, pushing and pulling our way through the dense jungle. It was as if there were numerous hands grabbing at our feet and our legs as we battled on. It was intense and bloody exhausting.

To make it more interesting, the afore-mentioned ants turned up. Large red bitey machines the size of small rats, biting their way through my clothes and up my trouser leg onto my bare flesh and digging their teeth in. Bitterly regretting my *executive decision* on the short socks, I had hundreds of these vicious arts gnawing away at my ankles, my calves and my thighs. Every bite was excruciatingly painful. What I would have done to have a pair of the Gorilla Agent's socks then.

By the time we stopped for our first break, two hours had passed. It was getting warmer and the humidity was rising. I was totally exhausted and so unfit.

Knew I should have trained for this.

The good thing was I had plenty of water and enough food to last me the five hours, or so I hoped. I spoke with the guide and was trying to work out how long it would be before we saw the mountain gorillas. From what I could understand he had little to no idea and we continued on deeper into the jungle and the mountains of the Congo.

We trekked for six more exhausting hours, having little rest breaks, with no sight of my teenage dream being fulfilled. No fucking mountain gorillas, just trekking, trekking and more trekking in the thick, now very hot and humid *jungle of death*, as I was beginning to think of it. The good news was the guide managed to find some gorilla shit that was about two hours old! This gave me some hope, but also did my head in; I just wanted to see the damn gorillas take some photos and get the hell out of there.

The rest of the trekkers were getting more and more anxious and frustrated with the guide. The whole situation, as was I, after several more blistering hours, came to a head. Within the space of about fifteen minutes my dream of seeing the "Rwandan" mountain gorillas came crashing down around me.

Resting in a very small clearing, we all confronted the guide and the two security guys, voicing our concerns about what was happening. The conversation got out of control very quickly, with all the shouting and screaming, it was rather dramatic. As it turned out, the main tool we had been using to navigate the jungle was the guide's small plastic GPS device, which he informed us in very broken English, had stopped working roughly four hours ago... *Fuuuuck!*

The jungle was quite dense and with the canopy covering any significant landmarks the guide had no way of figuring out where the hell we were. The situation was starting to become serious. We had been trekking for over eight hours and most of us only had barely enough food and water for five hours.

Suddenly the old American guy starting freaking out, like he was having some type of fit or seizure. For some reason, I rushed over to him and realized he was having a kind of hypoglycemic attack...

Could this trek get any worse? I thought.

Old man America hadn't eaten much food or consumed little water over the past eight hours because – wait for it – he and his daughter thought that food and drink would make their pack too heavy to carry...

The guy was shaking, white as a sheet and on the verge of passing out. He said that he felt his heart was racing out of control… Honestly, the first thought that came into my head was… *Stupid man!* But regaining some compassion I realized there was a very real possibility that something very serious was about to happen to him.

I laid him down on the jungle floor, trying to calm him down as much as I could. Then I remembered the hard sugar candies I had packed, so I jammed a few down his throat (half thinking they might actually choke him), gave him some of my remaining water and hoped for the best.

While I was doing this, his daughter thought she would freak out too, but only emotionally with an outburst of uncontrollable sobbing. The macho Aussie and the bookworm girl were sitting there very quietly, in a state of denial.

I knelt there beside old man America (trying hard not to think of how stupid he was) for a while trying to take in the situation in which I found myself. It was only supposed to be a five-hour trek and it was already pushing eight hours. The worrying thing was that we were deep in the jungle and logically, as it had taken us eight hours to get where we were and I was guessing it was going to be at least eight hours back to base camp. That's if we could find our way without the GPS. With no 7-Elevens or McDonalds out there, what the hell were we going to do for food and water?

From what I could work out, the guide and security guys still had no idea where we were either. I only had about a hundred milliliters of water left and the other thirst-crazed, manic trekkers had finished theirs a while back… The good news was, however, I had half a pack of cigarettes, five biscuits and four sugar candies left.

The guide notified us all – well from what I could work out anyways – to stay where we were and that he and the security guys would be back soon. And off they went, disappearing into the jungle. I believe they went out looking for higher ground to work out where we were. By this stage all of us were basically shitting ourselves, not knowing what the hell was going on or what was going to happen next.

I thought of the ridiculousness of our situation: *five Westerners stuck in the middle of the mountainous jungle of the DRC, all alone with no protection, next-to-no water or food, suffering from exhaustion and dehydration and in a fucking super-dangerous conflict zone.* Could this shit get any more out of control? Unfortunately, the answer to that was yes.

By this time it was three thirty p.m., which meant we only had about two, maybe three hours' maximum of sunlight left. Ask yourself, "Do you want to do dark in the DRC jungle?" This was something that I did not want to experience in any shape or form, ever! I managed to convince the group that it would be wise to try and make our way back to the base camp as soon as the guide and security guys returned. *If* they returned. (I guess those corporate team-building exercises were finally paying off.)

Waiting for over an hour, every minute felt like sixty, and I was getting more and more furious whilst the bloody paranoia was beginning to rear its ugly head within me.

Will they come back ever? What happens if the guerrillas with guns turn up? Or…What happens if old man America drops dead? There is no fucking way I am carrying a dead guy through the jungle back to base camp.

I tried very hard to breathe deeply and relax, sipping very slowly on the remainder of my water, knowing all too well the others were well on their way to dehydration and crazy town. None of them were in good shape: macho Aussie guy was showing signs of losing his shit at any moment, while the bookworm girl sat there staring into space with a look of dread. The nineteen-year-old Miss America was still sobbing and old man America was, well, just lying there.

So, this was what they meant by jungle fever.

I started hearing noises in the distance of tree branches breaking. My paranoia kicked like a crazed man screaming at me on a loud speaker, "It's the badass guerrillas coming to chop you up. We're all screwed, you're going to die!" Whatever it was, it was slowly coming closer and closer. I was essentially in a paranoid flat-spin with sweat pouring off me and my heart was thumping its way out of my chest. All my senses were pricked up like dog's ears on the hunt and I was solely focused on the rapidly approaching noise from the jungle which was directly in front of me.

Suddenly, out popped our frickin' guide, closely followed by the two security guys. I had completely forgotten they existed, clearly I was become more and more deluded. Feeling overwhelmed with relief to see them back, I immediately expressed the need to get the hell out of the jungle and back to base camp as soon as possible. Old man

America was not in good shape but had at least improved enough to sit up. Thank God for those sugar candies I had, as they seemed to suppress his symptoms.

After some heated negotiation with guide (not seeing the gorillas was not so good for his career I guess) he agreed to take us back and we set off. However, the guide clearly had no bloody idea which way to go as we all wandered through the jungle like lost sheep.

In my head, I began to try to come to terms with the fact that I wouldn't see the mountain gorillas. Despite the horrendous situation we found ourselves in, or maybe because of it, I was devastated. I had come so far. I was in their back yard; I could smell them – or their shit at least. *What a massive fuck up and missed opportunity.*

The dream had turned into a nightmare trek of life or death in the DRC jungle, and – *how little did I know* – what a nightmare it was going to be.

Trekking for the next hour it seemed we were going around in circles, up slippery verges only to fall down the other side into thick, unwelcoming jungle. I was constantly falling over and twisting my ankles, often landing on my tailbone just to add a little extra pain to the equation. The other trekkers were all now in full-on jungle fever mode, almost to the point of insanity. The girls were in tears, followed closely by the not-so-macho-now Aussie guy. Old man America was fairly much screwed so we had to keep stopping for breaks. As for me I was entirely inside my own head, completely pissed off and frustrated at the prospect of not seeing the mountain gorillas. I felt like I wanted to kill someone. My state of mind would soon deteriorate further as I became more and more dehydrated. Jungle fever had begun to set in for me too.

Sitting on the boggy floor of the jungle, totally drained, with the last rays of sunlight shining though the canopy above, I went to take my last tiny sips of water as the others stared and drooled at me. *Ow shit, I know I have to share, but really?* I thought. *Do I? It's my water!* I knew I needed to do the right thing; we were all in this together.

I handed the bottle with the last remaining water we had to the Aussie not-so-macho guy and as he put the bottle to his lips he let out a massive sneeze. Snot flew everywhere. I didn't know whether to laugh or cry as a large drip of snot plopped straight into the bottle of water. *Oh, seriously, that's just fucked up for the others,* I thought, but surprisingly they all had a sip in spite of it and quickly, our water supply was gone.

At this point we had been trekking for close on twelve hours and the terrain was at times almost completely impossible and more spirit-breaking with every step. Every muscle in my body was screaming in pain, my stomach was starting to eat itself alive and I could feel my entire physical being slowly drying up… To make matters worse, my back was completely screwed, and my left leg was only working intermittently.

Speaking with the guide again, he still was very unsure of where we were and he too was starting to buckle under the situation. It was getting darker by the minute, which ratcheted up the anguish in us all enormously. I guess we all knew that being in the jungle at night in the DRC would lead to a highly unfavorable outcome. No one dared speak a word about it but the terror was visible in everyone's eyes.

The guide indicated that it was time to get a move on, as we dragged our bodies onward into the jungle in the vain hope that we were heading in the right direction. I began to realize that trekking in the jungle at night is something of a brilliant nightmare. Every single cell in your body is pumping with alertness. The body's sensors are working overtime processing every movement around you and your inner survival mode kicks in as though you have reverted back to a caveman.

Stumbling through the thick undergrowth with the security guys up ahead hacking a path with their machetes, the feeling of functioning solely in survival mode began to grow within me and I was pushing the others to keep going, telling them constantly that everything was going to be ok. Perversely I was even starting to feel quite positive about the experience. However, this attitude didn't last long with the effects of total exhaustion and the serious effects of severe dehydration taking a firm grip.

Another two hours had passed and we were still nowhere – no base camp, no water, nothing. Feeling like I was chained to a never-ending jungle merry-go-round in hell, I was becoming more and more confused as to where I was and what the hell I was doing, and hallucinations were becoming an increasing problem for me. At one stage I found myself kneeling on the ground trying to ladle dirt into my mouth, thinking I was at the edge of a pond full of fresh, clean drinking water.

The other guys were about two stages ahead of me in terms of mental deterioration, which made things even more intense as I watched them slowly unwind into a state of pure insanity. We rested again and I remembered I had five biscuits left in my pack, so I shared them around to my fellow crazed, manic trekkers. *I need water and I need it now*, was all I could think.

As I bit into a piece of the biscuit, my tongue felt like it was twice its normal size as I tried to chew the biscuit. I was shocked to discover that I had no saliva left! I choked on half of it while the rest just slowly fell out of my mouth. I threw the remainder of the biscuit into the jungle and sat there shaking my head. At this point I had that dreaded, but by now familiar gut feeling. *This is my time to die. I'm screwed!* I thought. Exhaustion and severe dehydration had taken over, I had no energy and no fight left in me. I was on the thin line of letting life go. Kev was on my mind at this time and I guessed I would be seeing him sooner than I had previously thought.

It's hard to put into words the way that one feels when a situation becomes totally out of your control and death seems as though it's coming your way rapidly. The all-consuming feeling of complete helplessness and the total disappearance of all hope within was not in fact as frightening or alarming as you would imagine. If anything, it was quite calming. To let go of life itself and truly surrender and accept the situation at hand was kind of empowering and in hindsight this was the key thing that got me through.

The guide was looking totally overwhelmed, still not knowing where we were, and the security guys were getting more and more agitated with the situation, as well as with the five of us crazies. We continued stumbling and falling over through the thick mountainous jungle until suddenly... *Ow my lord!* We had finally reached the edge of the jungle from hell. It was about 10.30 p.m.

The whole group stood staring upwards in awe. We could finally see the sky and an impressive show of stars dimly lighting the landscape in front of us. I could just about make out some cornfields and another mountain range in the distance. Moving forward we came across a little mud hut and was hoping it included friendly inhabitants with water! The guide entered the hut and returned with an object, it was hard to see what it was until he got closer.

He approached us and held up the dark container. Fresh water! Each of us let out what seemed like a synchronized groan of relief as we all flopped onto the ground in utter exhaustion, in anticipation of our turn to taste this miracle. Drinking the water was possibly the most amazing thing I had done in many years, it was so spring-water-fresh; I could taste the pure nature in it. It was divine goodness.

We all rested near the little mud hut for some time, continuing to sip on the miraculous water till we felt we could make an attempt to move again. Our bodies were all but broken, but the water seemed to supply us with the hope that if we continued on we would somehow reach base camp and safety.

And so, feeling somewhat refreshed, we moved on through the fields leaving the scary, torturous jungle behind and started our ascent of the mountain range so the guide could try and get his bearings on higher ground. Reaching the top of the mountain range, again we let ourselves fall to the ground for a much-needed rest. My legs felt like boiling liquid was being pumped through them. I had managed to roll both my ankles several times and they were thumping with pain.

One of the other exhausted trekkers piped up, "Look over there, that's the sun setting." Way off in the distance there was another mountain range and I could see a bright, reddish glow emitting from one of the peaks and it looked so beautiful. Gathering my head together and realizing it was close to midnight, there was no way that was the bloody sun setting, that time was long gone. Trying to work out what the hell it was and trying even harder to focus on this bright reddish glow…

It was a frickin' volcano!

Sitting back and taking this all in was truly a remarkable moment. With not a cloud in the night sky, an amazing light show from the stars above and the bright reddish glow of the volcano, it made for a spectacular display. Sitting there, feeling much better about my disappointing and torturous 'non-gorillas-in-the-mist' ordeal, I realized that even with everything that had gone on, this sight had almost made it all worth it.

With a little smile of relief on his face, the guide informed us he was fairly sure where we were now, which was about 10 kilometers from base camp. Right at that moment my head span out of control and my heart rate hit the limit, my blood was boiling with anger. I couldn't physically walk, stumble or crawl another single damned kilometer, let alone ten. Then he finished with telling us that the road we came in on was about two kilometers away.

With this information, my whole body calmed, my heart rate lowered and relief washed over me. Just the thought of this day ending with everyone still alive was an overwhelming comfort. Getting our shit together we made the final push to the road. Arriving there at what had become the road of salvation, just about in one piece although scared with the day's and night's events and with a new-found phobia of jungles, we clambered aboard the little old Bongo van that turned up to take us all back to the border.

The Bongo van driver had been driving up and down the road for hours looking for us and he was totally pissed off, which was perhaps a little ironic given that we had until recently thought that we were about to lose our lives. Nonetheless, I was so happy to see his face, along with those of the two BSMF military guys next to him. The drive back to the border was the fastest Bongo van ride of my life.

Arriving at the border in record time, we were met with a very unhappy and worried group of people. The other travelers had been waiting there for us for about six hours. They had all seen the gorillas and had had a lovely day doing so. Looking all refreshed and a little concerned, they were relieved to see us back alive. It seemed that most of them had written us off as being killed or kidnapped.

The Gorilla Agent came over to our trekking group to ask how our day had been and to find out what we had thought of seeing the gorillas in their natural environment. This is when I totally lost my shit. I was still feeling the anger and sheer bewilderment of my teenage dream turning into a nightmare from hell.

I went off my head, literally frothing at the mouth. I told him we could have died or been killed out there, and that not only had we not seen any mountain gorillas but we had basically been wandering around the jungle lost for eighteen bloody hours! Once I'd started I couldn't stop ranting, all of my frustrations poured out. I demanded my money back. He stopped me mid-sentence to tell me that would never happen, although it was unfortunate, and he was sorry.

A very large scary looking local man approached and started accusing me of being full of shit, saying that in fact, we had seen the gorillas, and I was just trying to rip off Gorilla Agent. At this point, regardless of the size of the scary local man, I was ready to punch on. I was in an uncontrollable rage, I wanted blood! The scary local man demanded to see my camera for proof and I was more than happy to oblige.

I had four photos from our screwed-up, death-defying jungle adventure: a photo of some bamboo, a photo of the two-hour-old gorilla shit, one of the two-armed security guys complete with machine guns blowing me a kiss (humor was definitely called for at one point) and a frankly surreal group photo where we were all losing our heads at about the tenth hour of our living nightmare. The scary local man started to come around to the fact that I was telling the truth and with much reluctance the gorilla agent suggested we re-do the trek to see the gorillas in the next two days.

SERIOUSLY…?

"You want me to go back into the jungle again?" I exploded. I followed that up with, "You're totally out of your crazed head if you think I'm going back in there. You can stick your gorilla trek right up your ass."

I was on the verge of a full-scale meltdown, as some of the other travelers tried to calm me down. With all that had gone on before, my anger issues seemed to be spiraling into a particularly nasty place; clearly I needed to workshop my shit! But that would happen later.

I was slowly calming down to a warm idle as the Gorilla Agent explained that no money would be returned due to something about him having to pay the military and government up front but he offered to take us back personally to the mountainous jungle to view the gorillas in two days' time. He said that was the best he could do and asked me to think about it, along with the rest of my manic trekking companions. Something to think about? Or maybe not... The group had twenty-four hours to make a decision.

Maybe my dream is not dead after all, I thought. But do I really want to go back into that screwed-up situation again?

The next day, it was crunch-time!

Will I stay or will I go? I guessed with the Gorilla Agent with us, him being the main man, what could possible go wrong if I went back into the jungles of the DRC...?

I so badly wanted to see the mountain gorillas still, but at what cost to my mental and physical health? *Fuck it,* I finally thought, remembering that old saying, something about getting back on the horse. *I will go.*

Oh Lord... How little did I know what the DRC had in store for me in round two... *Ding... Ding!*

Ж Ж Ж

CHAPTER 11

DRC... ROUND TWO.

My alarm went off at 5a.m. Once again, it was time to prepare for the mountainous jungle of the DRC. It all felt too familiar and I was filled with apprehension about our return, plus my body was still hurting from the last trek. Knowing this time that the Gorilla Agent was joining us and as I said before, you would not want to cross this little man – he was well connected. We would be in good hands... I thought.

Arriving again at the border with the others, let's call them the *manic trekkers* (for sure we were for being willing to put ourselves through that again), we had an entourage of the Gorilla Agent's people fussing around us. It was like we were royal guests this time round. Unfortunately, this was not to last for long.

Once back in the DRC, we went through the same process as before, with visa approvals and paperwork. While waiting I had a chance to quiz the Gorilla Agent about why on the last trek our group had only had two armed security force guys. Thinking it would be a very straightforward answer, I instead got this, "Unfortunately there have been many problems in this region with the rebels. You were supposed to have another two armed security force guys, but they were shot and killed by the guerrillas four days ago while tracking one of the gorilla families." This got the heart rate up and going! And we were just about to walk back into this…

What the hell was I doing?

He went on to explain in detail the current situation with the guerrillas and how the National Park guides, the security guys and even the gorillas were being slaughtered on a regular basis in the region.

And for what, you might ask. For politically motivated agendas, the good old man-ego and the show of one's power. Such a truly horrible and sad scenario. (That's my limited and personal understanding.) After receiving this information I had a lot more respect for the guides and the security guys. To be in a position where you can be killed for simply doing your job – the job that you are very passionate about – and for trying to protect the politically oblivious mountain gorillas takes real courage. Amazing work guys.

My thoughts fell upon the question of my own mortality. In a few hours I would be potentially following in those guides' footsteps, once again in search of fulfilling my teenage dream. Feeling very uptight at this point, with my head madly processing the new and quite horrifying information, it was time to leave the border and head to the National Park's base camp to start a new adventure #2 in the jungle.

Sitting in the Bongo van for some time, I realized there was a problem. We had no military men to accompany us to the base camp. The upshot of this was, we could not move forward without their protection. The

Gorilla Agent informed us he was working on a solution and we had to wait at the border until that solution arrived.

Two hours passed and we were all getting quite edgy with the situation, so the Gorilla Agent did a deal with the driver to take us to a small village close by to wait for the military protection. Sitting in the van I could see the driver didn't want to move an inch without guards. I was sure this whole thing was going to end up in a massive shit-fight.

The 'laws of attraction' were flowing strongly that day for me and yes, the situation was about to turn into one of the scariest ones. That's apart from the *other* scariest experiences of my life I'd just had a few days earlier. Clearly, the DRC was not a good place for my mental health.

We left the border finally, that was, the other manic trekkers, the driver and the Gorilla Agent's main man. The Gorilla Agent assured us all that he would meet up with us on the way to the base camp and until then, his main-man would look after us. To make life a little more uncomfortable, the main-man happened to be the large, scary, local guy that had accused me of bullshitting about not seeing the gorillas and trying to rip off the Gorilla Agent. Yes, the very same man I had wanted to punch in throat at the border a few days earlier. He didn't seem too happy to see me. I hoped he had forgotten my little meltdown.

Bouncing along a little dirt track through tiny villages, again, the poverty was shocking. It was eye-wateringly intense. I was amazed at village life in the DRC compared to the well-oiled and shiny world that

I was used to. I felt like an alien in a strange new world. Furthermore, I was well aware we had no military protection – we were in the middle of a conflict zone. And there were more and more locals staring at us feeble white tourists. The tension and fear was rising steadily within the little Bongo van.

Suddenly our little, old Bongo van made a sharp turn, across a field and came to a stop in, well, I guess you could call it a village. It had about eighteen little huts and a main, very old, run-down Western style house in the center. The driver and the main-man got out of the van and walked off towards the run-down house. I was peering out the window.

Where the hell are we? I noticed a man coming out of the main Western style house in the middle with a machine gun hanging over his shoulder. The alarming thing was, while peering out the window I could see more and more of the local people coming out of their basic little huts and moving closer towards our van. None of the adults looked happy to see us Westerners in their neighborhood although the kids appeared more receptive and surrounded the van. I decided to get out too.

Leaving the safety of the van, I noticed the others were now all in a state of, 'what the fuck is going on?' I tried to talk with the kids, but it didn't work out too well. The kids were only interested in touching or pulling the hairs on my arms or staring at my green eyes, which seemed to freak them out.

It was as though I was a ghost; these kids made out like I was the first white person they had ever come into contact with. Meanwhile more and more of the adults were coming closer to check out the freak show of the "very scared white people in a van". The energy in the air was incredibly tense and was rising. It was like we were aliens and this was the first encounter: nobody knew if the other was a threat or not.

Quite clearly shitting myself with fear, the local adults had very aggressive expressions on their faces and it seemed they were not impressed with me interacting with their children. We were only making stupid faces at each other, as kids do, and I was trying to stay as passive as possible. My mind was going a million miles an hour though, processing all the information from this new environment and keeping a close eye on the local adults.

I was guessing that I didn't want to piss off anyone around here. I had a very strong gut feeling that we should not be there in this unknown little village somewhere in the DRC. This was evidently not a safe place for Westerners particularly considering we had no military protection, which the Gorilla Agent had previously insisted was paramount for our safety. I was still confused about why the hell he had organized for us to be dumped in the middle of frickin' nowhere!

Waiting for over an hour, with still no sign of our military escort, I was getting increasingly nervous and nature started calling. I needed to use the toilet and quickly. I walked over to the run-down house and asked the driver for directions, he just pointed at an old wooden shack about fifty meters away. While in the shack off-loading my nervousness into a hole in the ground, I looked out through the cracks in the wall and could see the whole village, including our van parked close to the run-down house. By this time the other manic trekkers were standing beside the van, and they all seemed totally freaked out by the situation and were being playfully harassed by the local kids.

Finishing my business, I took a final look through the cracks in the wall and saw that the number of curious locals had increased and they were even closer to the van. They were all standing perfectly still and staring at my fellow, manic trekkers as if they were in some bizarre zombie trance. I had a bone-chilling thought of watching the others being mowed down by machine gun fire and me being stuck in the shack, the only survivor to tell the story. The fear of what might happen was pumping through my veins like a fresh shot of heroin. My imagination was working overtime, if not completely out of control. Again, it was a situation of five feeble Westerners stuck in the middle of nowhere with no protection.

As I stumbled shakily out of the shack and made my way back to the van, it felt like the whole village was closing in on us. I had no idea what was going to happen next, but *holy shit*, things were not looking good.

Finally, the military men turned up with the Gorilla Agent in tow. *Thank God!* Still not sure whether they had been about to attack us or had simply been curious to see the freaked out white people in their village. I watched all the local people move back into their homes as the military arrived to save the day.

Is life all about timing?

Another hour had passed before the Gorilla Agent eventually got his shit together and finally it was time to move out of the scary little village. Now on our way to the great mountainous jungles of the DRC to see the gorillas, the atmosphere within the van had lifted a great deal and the light-hearted chitchat started. We were all very relieved to have the military and the Gorilla Agent with us again.

ЖЖЖ

CHAPTER 12:
DREAMS DO COME TRUE.

Arriving at the base camp, we started our trek once again up into the mountainous jungle but this time with a full entourage of military escorts, security forces, guides and the man himself, the Gorilla Agent. We trekked for about an hour before we came across the first signs of... the gorillas! *Holy shit,* I was so nervous, excited and overwhelmed at the prospect of meeting and spending time with the objects of my hard-fought teenage dream.

I will never forget the softly spoken words from the guide, "Just up ahead in the small clearing is a large family of gorillas, complete with a newborn and a silver back." I almost exploded with excitement over what I was about to witness. The guide gave us a quick brief on what to do when in the presence of the gorillas and off we went, buzzing like party-people coked off their heads.

Entering the small clearing it was like a true nirvana. The sun was gently shining through the trees onto the lush, green clearing, looking like a postcard from heaven, I was gob-smacked by what lay before me... the actual reality of my teenage dream! There were gorillas everywhere, eating, playing and farting. Yes, farting! Something to do with their diet.

Nineteen-year-old Miss America was standing up ahead as a young female gorilla rolled out of the thick jungle towards her and slapped her across the stomach! It was a priceless moment to see how these beautiful beings playfully connected and interacted with humans. It just so happened I had wanted to smack her and her father two days before for not packing enough food and water, but hey… that memory of the trek to hell was long gone. I was busy living out my dream!

I was so amazed at how close we could get to the mountain gorillas. There were no cement, steel or glass walls, they were literally right in our faces – to the point where they were actually trying to grab my camera out of my hands. We stayed with the gorilla family for about two hours, just sitting with them, witnessing their cheeky behavior and marveling at the dynamics of a gorilla family. I was total blown away; my expectations were met beyond belief. I was actually sitting in my dream, living it, feeling it and watching it all happen right in front of me.

I was kneeling with one of the guides, chatting about the mountain gorillas when two youngish female mountain gorillas rolled right in front of me fighting, with their teeth out. It was like some teenage disagreement. Their fighting continued for about two minutes. Then the sound of cracking and breaking branches just to the right of me got my attention.

Enter the big daddy… a massive silverback had arrived! He had come to break up the fight and restore peace in his family. He grabbed the two teenagers and pulled them apart. It was as if he was warning them, then sending them both to their rooms for time-out. I was so engaged with watching the silverback fulfill his parental role, it never even dawned on me that I had a colossal wild animal, twice the size of an average man, right in front of me. Amazingly, I had no fear at all!

Next thing I knew I had my head in the grass in front of me with a firm hand pushing on the back of my neck. It was the guide and he was repeating very softly, "No eye contact, no eye contact". Despite his very reasonable advice, I slowly raised my head and caught a brief look into the silverback's big, glassy brown eyes. He was such an amazing creation and so humanlike. It's said that our genes differ by only 1.6% from that of the mountain gorillas' and it was very evident. Slowly the silverback meandered off into the jungle to sit and watch over his beautiful family.

To spend precious time surrounded by the gorilla family in their environment, on their terms, in the mountains of the DRC was a once-in-a-lifetime experience, a dream come true. To be honest, sitting there, I was almost in tears. To think of what it had taken to get to this point in time: my little brother's suicide, my bullshit life back home and the trek from hell. I felt so blessed and grateful that life had led me to this point in time.

With our two hours with the grand mountain gorillas of the DRC up, we made our way back to base camp. The trek this time was like a Sunday stroll in the park. Mission accomplished; my teenage dream was finally realized.

ЖЖЖ

LESSONS LEARNT #4:

*"Take the good times with the bad, and
never be too quick to give up on your dreams.*

Failure is a great lesson in life that shows me what is truly important.

*I now use failure as a measure to what I think I honestly want. The more failure
I have and I still want it, I go get it"*

CHAPTER 13:
OUT OF AFRICA.

The next day was a ten-hour drive straight from the bowels-of-hell, in an even more beaten up Bongo van, with absolutely no comfort whatsoever on offer. The other travelers on the truck had moved on to another campsite and we needed to catch up with them. My adventures in Africa were fast coming to an end, which was a good thing in some respects, but I honestly did not want to face my homecoming, finding a new roommate or my bullshit corporate life. These things played on my mind for the remainder of the trip.

After a truly hellish ride in the Bongo *van of death,* we caught up with the other travelers on the truck and it was pretty much truck-travel life back to normal. The only country left on the tour was Tanzania, which was to offer one more enlightening experience on how things were done in Africa.

One late afternoon we arrived at our campsite in Tanzania and set up camp. The next day we were all going to the Ngoro Ngoro crater to do a safari and a 'free-camp', basically camping in the middle of the wild. We would take only the bare essentials, leaving the rest of our stuff on the truck, which was to stay at the current campsite.

The Ngoro Ngoro crater was one amazing place to hang out in for two days and the wildlife was intense. On return to the campsite where the truck was being kept, along with all our stuff, we were met with… No truck! And all our stuff was gone with it. *Oh the life of a traveler.*

The problem was the local police had heard we were in town and had come to check out the truck and driver's documents. The driver was from Kenya, which the locals did not like, so they threw him in jail and impounded the truck too. I was starting to think this trip was jinxed, *seriously!* Could anything else go wrong on my trip to escape my life back home? The solution to our problem was for the tour company to send a Western manager from the Nairobi office to Tanzania with a wad of U.S. dollars to pay off the police. *Bam!* Problem solved. With the truck and driver back, off we went again.

Heading for the coast, to the island of Zanzibar, everything was running smoothly, except that I had to face a very emotional date: my dead little brother's eighteenth birthday. Bloody crazy how life works – there I was in Africa attempting to run away from my past, but still my thoughts chose to turn to the very thing I was trying to escape. These were indescribably painful memories.

This made me stop and think of what could have been, had Kev not killed himself. If he was still alive, I would not have been in Africa, would not have seen the mountain gorillas nor would I have pretty much faced my own mortality. Life eh? You never know what's just around the corner.

The last port of call in Africa was to be the city of Dar es Salaam but before that I stopped at the island of Zanzibar. It is an amazing place, with the old Stone Town and its shocking history, spectacularly white sandy beaches and great coffee. It was a much-welcomed place to kick back, relax and reflect on my somewhat tormented adventures in Africa. I managed to have a few days on the beach before making my way to Dar es Salaam. This place was, in every way, the total opposite to Zanzibar; it was a sprawling, frightening, harsh city and I could not wait to get the hell out of there.

Leaving Africa, I was still in one piece (thank God!) yet slightly mentally and emotionally scarred from the experience – I was feeling very thankful for getting away with it all frankly. It was now time to enjoy Dubai and catch up with some friends. I was very excited about it, having heard loads about the place, and was looking forward to a little comfort after camping in some truly dodgy and wild places in Africa.

ЖЖЖ

CHAPTER 14:
THE DUBAI EXPERIENCE.

A rriving into Dubai from Dar es Salaam as a man travelling alone, baseball cap on and unshaven, in hindsight, I guess I looked a little drug dealer-ish. I made my way out of customs, thinking all was fine. From left field a young and very small security guy with a machine gun over his shoulder (which was almost the same size as him) startled me by grabbing me on the arm.

He wanted to know why I was in Dubai, where I had come from and demanded to see all my documentation. I was like, *'Seriously? What the hell is this all about?'* I just wanted to go to my comfy hotel, have a shower and relax. I felt like telling him all about my crazy adventures in the DRC in the hope that he might give me a frickin' break.

He checked my documentation and... *Oh no!* He ushered me off assertively to a little room. I was becoming more and more paranoid (as one would) and started racking my brain to think of things in my backpack that would cause me trouble.

Once in the little room, I sized up the tiny security guy and he looked, without a doubt, about twelve years old. I was being detained by a kid with a machine gun! He wanted to search me, which meant taking off all my clothes and standing there in my underwear. Every piece of luggage I had with me was opened and dumped on a table. This twelve-year-old went through everything – and I mean everything – every conceivable pocket and hiding place. Plastic bags, my socks, etc. – he even managed to find some hidden compartments within my backpack that I had never even seen.

These guys must have been trained from birth, he knew exactly what he was doing and if I actually had been a drug dealer or whatever he thought I was, nothing would have got past this tiny searching machine. The only thing he found was a small piece of Tanzanite (purple to blue gemstone) that I had forgotten I had purchased back in the northern Tanzanian city of Arusha.

He held onto my documents and the Tanzanite, told me to pack my stuff up and get dressed and then dragged me off to another room where a more senior security guy waited… I wondered if they were a father and son team, they looked so alike. The older guy fired off a few questions at me about my Tanzanite purchase and why I had not declared it, before going on to lecture me about bringing precious stones into Dubai. The old guy handed back my belongings and told me to get out of the room. I was finally free to go after three hours… *Welcome to Dubai!*

I was completely shattered by the time I got to the hotel. It had been a very long day. I had a sense of freedom, being in a safe and beautiful hotel with hot water and a comfy bed. It was heaven!

I had three nights in Dubai and what a crazy city it was – like the Wild West of the Middle East. Anything you wanted was on offer, but at a price. I went to some of those massive, overpowering malls to check out the shopping. It was totally in-your-face. These places are like temples for consumerism, every conceivable brand and outlet are there and as if shopping is not enough, you can actually go skiing in one of the mega malls.

I met up with my friends and they took me out on their very fancy speedboat to Dubai harbor. Waveboarding with the monolithic Dubai skyline as a backdrop was quite mind-blowing. This was the life! If you have money, you can have an amazing lifestyle here. It was so, so different to my four weeks of camping in wild and crazy Africa.

It was the last night of my mammoth adventure and I was feeling damn depressed. Within twenty-four hours I would be back to the monotonous day-to-day life that I had tried to run away from. No more camping, trekking or wildlife (or the opportunity to be shot in the face), just corporate bullshit, spreadsheets, paperwork and deadlines. Oh, and at some point I had to face the fact that my little brother was no longer there to hang out with. Added to that, I no longer had a roommate; just an empty apartment. I truly wanted to keep on running and running and running, I didn't want to go back to the life I had created or the lifestyle that I ironically thought was so important and good for me.

I was caught up in the type of lifestyle that always demanded more – more of anything and everything – it forced you into a state of mind where enough was not enough and status was everything. The more you had, the more you thought you were worth, yet that type of worth was truly hollow. *How little did I know?* Instead of realizing this,

I was going to dive headfirst back into this soul-fucking lifestyle and make several poor choices. I guess I was using it to escape from all the things I feared and needed to face in my life.

With what had happened in the DRC still fresh in my mind, I still wasn't sure how the hell I and the rest of the manic trekkers had gotten out of that situation alive. Luck or divine intervention? Or was I being saved for greater things to come? In fact, life was merely preparing itself to dish out some very brutal and cruel events in the near future. These were going to turn my life on its ass again and this time, truly bring me to my knees.

ЖЖЖ

LESSONS LEARNT: #5

"The world is indeed a crazy place of have and have-nots, with Dubai showing this in its full glory compared to Africa.

Going from the bare basics to anything I wanted, was an immense contrast of different worlds, yet still all run by that elusive dollar.

The arrogant gratitude I did practice was flawed. Now I see the real meaning of gratitude. To be truly thankful for what I have had, have and will have in the future, and more so my fortunate existence"

CHAPTER 15:
TIME FOR CHANGE OR KEEP ON RUNNING?

Arriving back home to a world without Kev, an empty apartment and my less-than-fulfilling lifestyle was such an anticlimax compared to the crazy shit that went on in Africa. The roommate had long gone, the pressure of my soulless career was back in my face and my little brother was just a memory. The last one played heavily on my mind every day, along with the fear of losing a clear memory of his face and the happy times I had shared with him.

Being back home and well into the daily grind, I was still not dealing with the immense tragedy of my little brother's suicide and how my life had changed because of it. I was not coping with all the emotions and, worse still, I was haunted by horrific nightmares nearly every night. These were nightmares about him being alive again and even though I knew he was dead; in my vivid nightmares he was so alive.

Running away to Africa had given me a much-needed break from my head and my heart. I guess that being so focused on staying alive and not being shot in the face helped. The biggest thing had been having the space to think without being constantly reminded by my surroundings that Kev was dead. Now, back to reality, I needed to find something to keep the distraction going. I had no idea what to do with pain and the all-encompassing feelings of loss. How do you deal with that shit? Run and hide? Medication or therapy? The latter was coming, but not the conventional kind.

I decided I would throw myself into my soulless career; I would work as much as I could and start studying too. The idea was, the more time I spent focused on my soulless career and studies, the less time I would have to pay attention to my ever-growing emotional pain, which was sucking the life out of me. The upside of this was also that I could earn loads of money and hopefully buy myself some inner peace, if needed and needed it was.

In my new, numbed state of existence not only working crazy hours but studying to complete my diploma in business management, I had another idea. I would buy my first property. I thought this would make my life more stimulating and further improve my "status" by fulfilling another whim. I was, at the time, renting an old Victorian-style apartment which had far too many memories of the old good life I had once lived, so to speak. The apartment was where Kev used to come and hang out, and where he had lived with me for a while. It was a place of laughter, happiness and funny times.

Coming home every day to this empty apartment with just the stale memories of what had once been, was not a pleasurable thing. I needed to get the hell out of there and attempt to start new memories in another place. Or was I just running from my painful past?

My career was on track financially, although it was eating away at the very core of me bit-by-bit, day-by-day. I was at least fortunate enough to be in a position where I could purchase an apartment, with some short-term financial assistance from my mother, surprisingly. I had been reading many books, from property to spirituality (hippy shit, as I affectionately called it) and had found a very interesting book entitled *The Secret*.

It was all about the laws of attraction, which interested me greatly, and I started trying to work out how to put what I was learning into action. Reading the book, it all seemed so easy – any half-educated person could master this skill. Looking back on my past and all the shit that had gone on, I honestly wanted to step far away from all the suffering and focus on some positive changes for myself.

Clearly, I did not want to face my past at that time – I only had the ability to run from it, although some five years later, while living in Barcelona, my past was going to harpoon me.

The weird thing was, the more I ran, the more the bad shit would happen, as though I was like a massive negativity-shit-magnet. This was seriously screwing with my head and it was time to attempt some changes in my life or start running faster!

I started reading more and more about these so-called laws of attraction, becoming intrigued by the whole concept. I was starting to look further into the hippy shit stuff. I had always been quite interested in it and with my experiences with Kev and Africa, I was beginning to open up to the possibilities of entertaining other aspects of the world I thought I was living in.

One night I imagined the exact apartment that I wanted and wrote it all down, right down to the price, location, features and local services. I tried in the coming weeks to think, live and breathe what I had read in *The Secret*. With the soulless career, studying and now my newfound interest in real estate, I was on a new track. Unfortunately not the right one, just a new one.

The right path would be shown to me later. However, I needed to be smacked in the face a few more times by life, so I would open my eyes up properly, to then see clearly where I needed to go. Oh, yes, I was going to learn and it was going to be a hard lesson until my eyes were fully opened.

ЖЖЖ

CHAPTER 16:

UPPING MY "STATUS" AND SACRIFICING MY SOUL.

Madly working away at my career one afternoon, pumping out the usual corporate crap on the computer, I stopped for a moment. I quickly checked the local real estate website. Scrolling through the pages of properties, one apartment felt like it literally jumped out at me. I sat there with my heart racing and my face stuck to the computer screen, scanning the page for all its information.

Without a second thought, I picked up the phone, called the agent and set a time to meet and view the property. *This was the one.* It was just as I had written about using the theory of the laws of attraction. Again, without any real thought I made an offer on the spot and much to my surprise, within two hours it was accepted. I was amazed at how with a little focus I could attract things I thought were important into my life. However, I was in for a rocky relationship with this new theory. It is certainly true… You are what you think.

Two months later I found myself sitting in my newly purchased apartment, somewhat astonished at the speed by which it had happened. The only thing missing off the list I had written was a gas cooker. My must-have-everything lifestyle was coming together and

my illusory status was rising as I accumulated more material things…
I was starting to feel encouraged; life was not so bad after all.

And so the task of packing up my life and moving it to a new place
began. Putting a whole apartment into boxes again for a second time
in less than ten months was no fun at all, but this time it was about
new beginnings and not the end of a loved-one's life. Although saying
that, letting go of the old apartment and all the good times that I had
had there was damn hard. The hardest thing was coming across things
that Kev had left behind on past visits, and it was heart-wrenching
finding old handmade birthday cards from him when he was only five
or so. Call me crazy, but I always found it hard to let go of things, and
particularly people.

While that was all going on, the management at work in their wisdom
had realized that I was not so stupid after all and decided to promote
me to the position of Sales Manager for the region. I was a little
apprehensive to start with, yet the possibility to further improve my
deluded scene of the status I believed in, outweighed any fears. The
thing was, the company was owned by about five guys, kind of like
a family business and at times very much a boys' club. I got on well
with most of the owners, though I did have some run-ins with one or
two of them, like my old *friend* Bald Ego. He was a thirty-something,
uptight, egomaniac. Looking back, I think he too was stuck on the
same bullshit lifestyle path as me.

The main guy running the company was – let's call him the *Smiling
Assassin*. That pretty much sums him up. I always thought we had a
solid and genuine working relationship. It's funny how you can think

you understand the complexities of relationships in the corporate world, only to realize you have no frickin' idea! That was basically the case my whole corporate life and to some extent in my personal life too. It's all smoke and mirrors, with the addition of a few games and the bullshit of politics thrown in to keep you on your toes. Makes for a damn complicated life.

Seriously! Isn't life hard enough without all that crap?

The company in which I worked was becoming a formidable force in the cutthroat world of Information Technology Services. It was the era of sell, sell, sell, at all cost! And the industry was overflowing with "cowboy" sales guys, which made my career even more destructive. These cowboy sales guys would sell their own grandmothers. There were masses of dodgy deals going on all over town, across all levels of business and some of these cowboys and the companies, which employed them, were making millions.

I was not one of the cowboys, my hippy side always made sure ultimately I was at least honest and did the right thing, regardless of the money. If only I could have cut out the integrity within me, I would have become a very successful and rich man (financially, anyway).

The company I was with was playing the dodgy corporate game very well, so I found out. Being a sales manager, I had access to numerous financial reports and the numbers were not even close to adding up.

What the hell have I got myself into? I remember thinking. The whole situation made my skin crawl: the lies, the games and the lack of basic human respect. They say you become like the people with whom you spend the most time. The fact was, I was struggling – it was dog-eat-dog, an egomaniac's paradise, and I didn't have the ignorance to enjoy it.

To make matters worse, I was also a borderline "Type A" personality kind of guy: everything had to be done right the first time, yet I knew once completed, I could do it even bigger, better and quicker the next time round. This frustrated the hell out of me. I was an out-of–control, continuous-improvement junkie. Everything had to be perfect and completed yesterday, but working in a large, family-run company I was continually pissing people off with my anally retentive attitude. It was quite surprising how most people would settle for mediocrity.

In full fight as a "Type A" Sales Manager, I had upped my status once again and my chosen bullshit lifestyle was coming together, for the time being. Later it would become, well, not-so-together. I was working twelve to fourteen hours per day, most weekends and had basically no social life – it was all aboard the corporate-burn-out train and I had first class tickets! As I said, life was in the process of teaching me some cruel yet valuable lessons.

One of the lessons was to truly understand the people closest to you in the corporate world, know where you stand with them and not get caught up in office politics. You know the story, 'he said, she said' crap that goes on in office life. I still cringe at the thought of it all – it blows me away where the hell some people get the time to practice this modern-day art form. Image if those people focused the same kind of energy on the job at hand… What a different world we would live in!

I was managing a team of alleged sales professionals – some great and some not so great. Putting my heart and soul into my new role was not enough, the owners and managers kept asking for more and more, on all levels, and Bald-Ego was trying his hardest to make my life hell any which way he could. Honestly, even from my "Type A" stand point it was a mistake taking on the Sales Manager role. Think Obama taking over from Bush kind of deal.

I went about my business very openly and honestly, I was not related to the owners and I was far from being in the exclusive "inner" boys' club of the company. I was an outsider, meaning, the first hint of trouble and I was doomed! The things you do, just to have "status" in the corporate world.

The most important team member, as it turned out, was the Smiling Assassin's son, and what a total headfuck he was! An eighteen-year-old smart-ass that knew everything, yet at times he was a somewhat likeable kid. He had been in every department in the business and was finally off-loaded onto the sales team. This was where I came unstuck, with some help from another team member – the *Coke-snorting Stalker guy*. The Smiling Assassin told me several times to be honest with him while managing the team. I believe I was… perhaps too honest at times, which caused no end of trouble for me.

Managing the Smiling Assassin's son was a full time baby-sitting gig; every day there was a drama and every day I was there to assist and resolve it. I spent hours helping and guiding this kid, however it was like pushing shit up a hill with a stick! Behind the scenes he was reporting back to the Smiling Assassin and basically dumping on anything and everything I was doing.

I was solely focused on the greater good of the company... How stupid was that? Looking back it feels as though I was doomed to fail in this family-run free-for-all. I was no blood relative and I should have been focused on learning the fine art of kissing ass or ego massaging! Lesson: blood is thicker than water and in a family run business, regardless of whether the kid was a totally out-of-control, mendacious brat; his words had much more value.

It didn't matter the amount of training, experience and education I had. For over fourteen years I had been in the IT sales and marketing world and had seen it all, but not this... Such high school crap. As for the Coked-up Stalker, he was on a path to self-destruction, but he had one skill that I so badly lacked, kissing the asses and massaging the egos of the senior managers and the owners. This guy was at times brilliant, yet drugged up to his eyeballs most days and took customer service to a new level by repeatedly having sex with clients and then stalking them. Maybe a hobby would have been a better way to spend his time, or even having a go at doing his job properly.

I made the key owners aware that he was out of line, yet not giving away too much detail of his additional services to the clients or his coke habit. Sadly my revelations were not welcome and were brushed aside. This guy was making my career ever-so-interesting every day. Being coked off your head, you tend to forget what you say and do, so the bullshit was running thick and fast. I was trying every-which-way to manage this guy – remember it was sell… sell… sell! Meeting sales targets monthly were "king" and I was coming up short every time with this guy and the kid. And no results effectively meant I was not doing a good job.

The Coked-up Stalker managed to have the owners in his hot little hands and could do no wrong in their eyes, yet I was an over-reacting manager that was not performing. The classic saying "can't see the trees from the forest" somewhat sums up the situation with the owners, and I guess for me too. So, with the kid and the Coked-up Stalker undermining anything and everything I did, my days as a sales manager were numbered. Plus, by this time my health was beginning to unravel under the added stress and pressure.

If only I had been using my newfound interest: the laws of attraction. However, at the time I was struggling to keep my head above water and the majority of my thinking revolved around the fact that I believed I was not good enough and I was going to fail. I was beating up on myself and the wheels of my deluded lifestyle and career were starting to fall off! It was time for some long overdue outside help.

ЖЖЖ

CHAPTER 17:
ENTER THE GURU-GUY.

With my career, life and health all starting to come apart at the seams, life was clearly telling me to seek some much-needed professional help. At the time I was popping anti-depressants like candy in the hope they would hold off a complete mental meltdown. My ego was not happy about seeking help of any kind – it just wanted to keep on going on as normal. Deep down I knew it was time to face up to myself, the situations I was running from and the ones I had also worked so damn hard to get myself into.

I met with my doctor. Doc-B was a good guy. Late thirties, well adjusted for a doctor and a total techno-gadget man. He had every damn medical gizmo money could buy. I think he had a liking for me. Or maybe he just felt sorry for me, either way he was a great guy to have on my side, which is something everyone needs sometimes. This is something I had learnt in previous years and would learn further as my life unfolded into something resembling a bucket of steaming shit.

Doc-B and I talked for over an hour about my life, Kev's suicide and my health. Plus, the fact that I was not coping with the pressures of maintaining my desired status, or the bullshit of corporate-land. In those moments, sharing my thoughts and feelings with another was kind of comfort yet my ego was incensed by the weakness I was showing. It was demeaning to ask for help or even admit that I was failing and not coping with life. It didn't really fit my outward appearance as a "corporate executive".

Doc-B referred me to a therapist he believed would give me some guidance, which would help me to wade my way out of my mental maelstrom. He did warn me the therapist was not the conventional type and he was a somewhat unique individual from another country. From this I had no idea what to expect; the image of a three-headed therapist with too many arms came to mind. Doc-B wanted me to up my meds too, in the hope of settling my crazed, merry-go-around-mind further.

I was feeling rather disturbed because every time Doc-B changed the anti-depressant meds it would take several weeks, if not months, for my body to adjust. That in itself was enough to tip the sanest person over the edge. Walking out of Doc-B's office I was on the verge of an anxiety blowout, I had just agreed to start therapy with some three-headed, multi-limbed guy! *What the hell was I doing?*

Walking down the street, I remember thinking… It's one thing to think about my issues in the safety of my own head, it's another thing talking about them out loud to a therapist. I had already learnt that once my issues were out in the open they would take on a life of their own, like a dead horse tied to me that I had to drag around.

Was I about to open a big old black hole of pain and bullshit that I could not close?

And before I knew it, it was time for my first session and I was shitting myself, full of anxiety and fear in the knowledge of what I might have to face. I raced from my life-sucking-career in my designer suit across town to the therapist's office. To make matters worse, or more interesting I guess, his offices were in the down-and-out part of town, his neighbors were drug users and prostitutes wandering around the streets looking for their next hit or client. This was a little disturbing, yet it made me feel my issues may not be so bad after all. It's funny, when you think your life is a bucket of shit, there is always someone else with a bigger bucket.

Sitting in the run-down waiting room, there was no receptionist – no other people at all in fact, just two old chairs, a pile of out of date magazines, a door to another room with an overpowering smell of stale cigarettes. I was trying to get my crazed head together so I could explain to the therapist that my life was a big steaming mess and I was falling apart. My anxiety was fluctuating from "I'm ok" to "I'm about to explode".

I'm ok, I thought again. And almost simultaneously, *I'm going to run out the door any second!*

I could faintly hear people talking in the other room when the door opened abruptly and out came a thirty-something guy in tears closely followed by an old-looking Indian guy.

Enter the Guru-Guy! The unconventional therapist I had been told to expect was the old Indian guy. He was in his late fifties, overweight, with thick grey hair and beard, dressed in 1970s-looking clothes.

Despite his surprising appearance, he had a very calming presence about him. I later found out he was well travelled, studied many cultures and religions. Oh, and a fully committed chain-smoker. The good news too was he only had one head and two arms so I relaxed a little. Even better, he truly knew his stuff about life and people with problems, which was great for me…

He gestured to me to come into his office, which was virtually the same state as the waiting room but with a more of an intense smell of stale cigarettes. We both sat opposite each other in big old green leather armchairs. With complete silence and me frozen in a state of… "What the hell do I say to this guy?" Guru-guy gently leaned forward and with a soft Indian accent asked, "What are you doing here and how can I help you?"

I could feel that half-dead horse start tugging at my neck. I just sat there staring at him, completely blank, trying to get my brain into gear and spit out some kind of understandable response. To be honest I had no damn idea what I was doing there at that moment, I was slowly sinking into denial and had managed to convince myself I was fine, life was great and I needed to run and run quickly!

The last time I was in therapy was to face up to my childhood and the heartbreaking and soul-fucking reality that a family member had fiddled with me as a kid, not in a good way. That process near killed me and I nearly killed myself; it was a lot to face up to and make peace with. Now I was back in that same environment, facing up to my life and I needed to give Guru-Guy an answer.

I spluttered out that I was barely keeping my life together under the pressures of my career, failing health and the crippling grief of Kev's suicide. This took a while to explain and Guru-Guy just sat there very calmly, nodding his head from time-to-time and taking some notes as I verbally spewed out my emotions. The 'black hole' was officially opened and the flailing of the half-dead horse had started! I was finally facing up to what I needed to and once I had started, it all flowed out.

I would see him twice a week and basically offload all my emotional shit onto him, yet he would sit in his big old green leather armchair and reply only with a few words, in his soft, wise, Indian accent. Guru-Guy's few words were always so directional and inspiring, like a spray of cool water in the face on a hot day; so refreshing.

One thing that happened to me through spending more time with Guru-Guy was that I stopped looking outwards for answers and started looking within myself… Well some of the time anyways. I was officially on some pathway to hippy-land or at least becoming more aware of what was going on inside my head and the world around me.

As time went on Guru-Guy managed to drain more and more crap out of my head, which in turn freed up some space so I could think clearly and try and live a "normal" life, so to speak. Probably one of the most eye-opening and thought-provoking books he suggested I read was The Power of Now by Eckhart Tolle. It was all about living in the present moment without all the crap that goes on in your head – thoughts of this or that – and understanding how the ego mind works.

Reading this book like a self-obsessed hippy, at first I had no frickin' idea what the hell I was reading and struggled to even comprehend living life in the present moment. I was so committed to thinking and living in the past or the future... Maybe to protect myself, who knows? The idea you could live in the now was a total 'brain freeze' to me at the time. I was a recovering thought-aholic and needed further support and a shit load more sessions to be properly cured.

The more sessions I had with Guru-Guy and the more I read *The Power of Now*, the more I grasped the theories of Eckhart Tolle. Life started to become a little easier to understand and to accept. To be honest the Guru-Guy and the teachings of Eckhart Tolle truly changed my life in the short term, and to an extent forever. But I still found it incredibly hard to accept many things in my life. Especially the suicide of Kev and parts of myself. I still had so many "why" questions unanswered, which played on my mind daily.

With my new knowledge in hand and some new skills sinking in for coping better with life's situations, I ventured head-first back into the material world and straight back to feeding my deluded lifestyle. I was kind of thinking that I was o.k. and could have the best of both worlds: money, status and some hippy stuff to make me feel spiritual or connected to something greater than me.

However, I had more lessons to learn and life was going to throw some nasty curve balls my way in the coming years. How little did I know...? My life was about to hit some very serious turbulence once again.

ЖЖЖ

LESSONS LEARNT: #6

"The power of a mentor's guidance. The following quote blew me out of the water and had a profound impact on my business and personal lives.

'You don't know, what you know'

Simple yet powerful, it hit my ego like a truck and made me look at learning in a totally different light."

CHAPTER 18:
A NEW YEAR… A NEW START?

It was a new year, and all I could think was, *thank God 2007* is over. It had been one of the hardest years of my life and full of too many surprises. Some good ones but unfortunately the bad ones seemed to take precedence… Well in my head anyways.

Going through the Christmas and New Year period without Kev for the first time and just a memory of the previous Christmas where we were all together as a family, hurt like hell. I found myself living in the past, trying to hold onto a fading feeling of Kev still being alive and ignoring the fact that he was long gone. I guess this time of year can be hard for some people, facing families or being alone or just the pressures of the season.

It was also one year since Kev's suicide and this brought up even more emotions that I was not ready to face. Yet people around me wanted to remind me of this anniversary. I still had no idea how to deal with Kev's suicide; I just wanted to disregard all the emotional bullshit and push on with my life. I was trying to stay focused on the positives and use what I had learned from the Guru-Guy.

Again, I just threw myself back into my career and was looking for ways to up my status further to numb the pain so I could feel good about life and myself. I was thinking a new year, a new start and it would be full steam ahead. The next step in fulfilling my deluded sense of status was to buy a sports car. Every up-and-coming corporate Sales Manager needs a sports car to go with the warehouse loft apartment.

Due to my crazy career hours, studying and just starting renovating my apartment, I had no time to look at new cars. Being in IT and connected 24/7 had its pluses so I popped online late one night and ordered myself a brand-new sports car, complete with finance and delivery to my apartment. Too easy! So now I had it all, I had the desired life, I was living the dream and my status was all but complete. I guess people looking at my life from a distance would think I had it all, materially anyways. Yet no one could see that half-dead horse of misery I was dragging around.

Superficially I was on track and surprisingly happy. Things had settled down somewhat with my career and I was making some headway with management and the owners. On the family front my sister with her family had decided to move to Samoa of all places, where her husband had taken up a job. Although I was kind of losing another family member it was only a five-hour flight away and I was planning on visiting them at Easter time... Life was pretty good, or so I thought.

...

Party season was coming up in Sydney and my friends were working out what parties to go to. The old roommate, who was a great mate, was back in town and had just moved into a dodgy little apartment in the inner city, party central. It just so happened that it was right on the route for one of the biggest street parties in the world, The Sydney Gay and Lesbian Mardi Gras. If you want crazy, this party has it all and generally goes for days.

The Sydney Gay and Lesbian Mardi Gras starts with a parade through the streets of Sydney and on a good year you may get close to a million people from all over the world visiting the city and taking part in the parade. I have many friends from all walks of life and so many times they have tried to get me to go in the parade, but it just was not my thing. How little did I know, not only was I going to have a starring role in the parade but also would manage to stop it in its tracks!

All my friends decided to attend the parade and after-parties – we planned to view the parade from my old roommate's new place. To be honest I didn't want to go at all, I had had a hellish week at work, was super tired and run down but, at the last minute I thought, what the hell! What else would I do? Stay home and watch a movie while the city parties? On the way there I got a weird-assed feeling, you know those feelings you get from time-to-time that something is not quite right?

I got to my old roommate's place. All the streets were blocked off and there were people everywhere dressed up in fancy party clothes and some not so dressed at all! The fun had started and it was time for one of the world's largest street parades to get under way. The atmosphere was intense with fireworks, loud music and people screaming with excitement everywhere. I managed to find a great place to watch the parade on a temporary balcony kind-of-structure with a few friends and a vodka in hand.

About an hour into the parade while taking in the sights and sounds, enjoying the night and thinking… "WOW, this is great fun, so many people going crazy, sucking up the atmosphere and partying hard." I was chatting with two beautiful ladies who I had just met and they were telling me all about how they had recently got married. They were so in love and incredibly happy to be with each other, it was awe-inspiring. It made me wonder who had the right to deny two people in love their right to marriage. I guess that's a sticking point for many, yet I am sure there are more important issues in the world that could be dealt with and honestly, who gives a shit who marries whom anyway? I think Australia is a little backwards with the whole same-sex marriage thing. Let's hope one day all have equal rights and there is an end to religion and politicians telling people who they can or cannot love.

Anyways, I was so engrossed with the parade and my newfound married friends when a rather camp young man jumped onto the balcony and starting bouncing around like he was having some type of fit. It turned out he was dancing. A few people asked him to calm down or get off the balcony, yet he continued knocking into people and dancing like a total dickhead. As I got that feeling again that something not so good was about to happen, the balcony shook a little under my feet.

I was standing near the edge of the balcony with my newly married friends facing me, we all leaned forward to gain our balance again and then the balcony shook some more and ever so slowly it started to collapse under our feet. I remember trying to grab hold of something, anything and looking into the eyes of the women. Their look was of sheer panic as they stumbled towards me sympathetically pushing me off the balcony backwards.

It was as though the whole universe went into slow motion for a moment as I fell. Looking back into the faces of the people that were about to follow me over the edge, I thought… 'this just can't be fucking happening!' Then a clear voice with in my head said, "be like a cat" so I twisted around to my right as I fell, trying to land on all fours, so to speak – like a cat. To this day I have no idea where or what the voice was, if I had not twisted you would not be reading this book as I would more than likely be dead now.

I hit the ground hard, right arm first, bounced and skidded on my side along the cement to a stop as the others followed mostly landing on their feet. It was like a human avalanche and thank God they all missed landing on me! I rolled over and lying there flat on my back staring up at the sky in some considerable pain, I could hear people screaming and crying. Yet I had a very surreal calm feeling as the universe popped back into normal speed.

Holy shit! I was still alive! In pain, but alive. Out of the corner of my eye I could see the owner of the building racing towards me with a camera in hand. He was shouting at me and taking photos of the situation, including me lying on the ground helpless. He continued rambling and shouting about something to do with insurance, I was a trespasser, I was o.k. and needed to get off his property.

I just wanted to punch the guy in the head. I could see his little angry face, I think I even had a few swings at him with my left arm; clearly I was in shock and going nowhere fast. My friends pushed him away and a small fight broke out with him, people yelling and screaming for him to fuck off! And finally he did.

My old roommate knelt down beside me trying to figure out how bad I was; I could see in his eyes the distress that things were not looking good. He tried to sit me up with not much success… I could feel my legs, back and arms, but while lifting me up my right arm just stayed still on the ground. I slowly lay back down with the realization that I had basically broken my right arm off from just below my shoulder; the only thing holding it together was some skin and muscle.

That's when everyone freaked out and starting screaming even louder to call an ambulance; it was totally out of control. The other people that fell seemed to have got away with only minor injuries or maybe they had just drunk more than I had. I was the unfortunate one, falling backwards onto cement from three meters isn't good for one's health, as I found out.

The surprising thing was: no head damage! Not a bump or scratch to be found. Well my arm was totally smashed and I had skid marks up the right side of my back, but other than that I was fine and more importantly, I was alive.

Lying half-stunned with people staring down at me with very concerned faces, the pain started to set in slowly and all I wanted was a cigarette and maybe another ten or so vodkas! My old roommate handed me a cigarette and with my left hand I starting smoking, staring at the night sky with people carrying on partying and the parade still passing nearby. I tried to keep calm, waiting for the ambulance and paramedics to arrive.

After about fifteen minutes three or four paramedics arrived with all their emergency equipment and starting fussing around me. Then the twenty questions started, are you ok? Where is the pain? Can you feel this or that part of your body? Have you taken any drugs? They asked that about ten times. By this point in my life I was drug free and had barely had two drinks since arriving! But the thought of some drugs seemed like a damn great idea by that point.

The paramedics starting looking at my right arm, poking around, getting me to wiggle my fingers and move my hand. They looked all very concerned and started explaining to me that I had smashed my upper arm and elbow but everything else seemed to be in the right place.

It just so happened I was wearing my all-time favorite shirt, one that I had had tailor-made while travelling in Vietnam, yes, the same trip where I vomited and almost shitted myself to death. The paramedics wanted to cut my favorite shirt off me and I was like… *Noooooooooo!* "It's my all-time favorite shirt, please… please… please don't cut my shirt." This made me so pissed off! I was at a party-parade thing I didn't want to go to, I had just fallen off a balcony breaking my arm off as I went, and now my favorite shirt was going to be hacked off me. Could this night get any worse?

I watched them slowly hack off my shirt and I was thinking it would be fine, I could get it repaired later… But I never saw that shirt again. This left me lying there flat on my back half naked. I guess I fitted in more now with the party-parade theme. I was so pissed off about that shirt though.

It was time to move me and get me to hospital, they immobilized my arm with some fancy blow-up plastic thing, put me on a gurney and stuck a large tube in my mouth and told me to suck on it for pain relief. *WOW* it was amazing; I was completely off my head within seconds and feeling so free and blissful. My old roommate was standing next to me so I gave him a suck on the tube so we were now both off our heads and having a laugh.

This didn't last long. I started to lose my shit; basically going into an emotional flat-spin with the growing comprehension of what was happening. Also, being that drugged off my head opened my mind to the true pain and grief of Kev's suicide and it just all gushed out of me. It was uncontrollable gut-wrenching crying and in all honesty… right at that moment I just wanted to be dead – to be with my little brother in a better place and not off my head lying on a gurney with my arm hanging off.

To make things just a little more interesting, the only way to the ambulance was along the road where the parade was taking place. So, the paramedics got the police to stop the 2008 Gay and Lesbian Mardi

Gras parade in its tracks. Then two paramedics and my old roommate push me down the parade route with thousands of partying people looking on. Oh, and the whole parade was being broadcast live to millions too!

Ironically some of my friends got their wish and that was how I made my Mardi Gras parade debut. Lying on a gurney, half naked, off my head-on pain relief and crying my eyes out wishing I were dead. Not ideal and probably one of the most humiliating moments in my life but, that was nothing compared to the next few weeks in hospital.

ЖЖЖ

CHAPTER 19:
MORE PAIN RELIEF... PLEASE!

Waking up the next day in a stark white room, small plastic tubes now hanging out of my arm left arm and my right arm strapped to my chest, I was totally confused. I had no idea where I was or what the hell was going on. I was drugged to the eyeballs still, this time with morphine straight into my vein and I had a little button I could press to have a dose of bliss whenever I wanted it. So, there were *some* positives!

It took me a while to realize I was in hospital and then slowly I started to remember the goings-on from the night before. The party, the parade, the people and oh shit... the human avalanche! I closed my eyes and wished it were all a bad dream, hoping when I opened them again I would be safely in the comfort of my own bed.

I was in hospital and I just lay there staring at the ceiling vaguely wondering what was going to happen next before I nodded off to sleep.

When I came to, I was for some reason in the cancer ward with many sick and dying young people and my old roommate was one. It was quite a sobering experience considering the night before I came very close to losing my own life and then wishing I were dead while at my Mardi Gras debut.

I guess it was the first time my defenses were fully down after Kev's suicide and the true pain of that was unbearable to live with. I remember thinking as the intense and consuming pain flowed through every cell of my being that I just wanted to be dead, and the want was as strong as the pain. This scared me somewhat and I wondered if I too would take my own life at some point in the near future or would the hippy-shit take me in a different direction?

But for now, I needed to get my arm stuck back on and quickly. I had a career and a lifestyle to get back to. My brand new sexy sports car was going to be delivered within weeks; I had no time for injuries and hospital bullshit. I needed help and fast but I was in no state to deal with doctors, specialists and all the paperwork. I couldn't even write; I was right-handed and that was strapped to my chest. Also, I could barely see I was that high on morphine. Damn I love morphine!

My old roommate must have rung around letting family and friends know what had happened because slowly but surely the visitors started arriving to check out my latest situation. Two good friends went to my house and got some of my personal stuff, more importantly my laptop and Blackberry. I needed to be connected; I was only thinking about my career and knew I could not be offline for too long. There were shitloads of work to be done; reports to write, clients to contact, people to manage and sales targets to hit, or I would be in deep shit.

This is what I was thinking the whole time. Career, career, career. But it turned out I was in worse shape than first thought. The doctors and specialists called a meeting with my family and me the second day in hospital to inform us that I had literally shattered my elbow and upper arm – it was all in little pieces. They had no idea how they would piece it back together but they were working on a solution and would operate within five to seven days.

It was like my life was over... if I couldn't get back to my bullshit career in the next seven days I would be crucified by management. And I was nearly spot on! By day two or three I was moved to the orthopedic ward and the phone calls started. The Smiling Assassin was demanding to know when I would be back in the office. He was so pissed off with me. I think he thought I was just lazing around at home with a simple broken arm, more than capable of working. His attitude on the phone just underlined the fact there was not much care and I was just part of the system. This nail was going to be driven home further in the coming months with his and others' actions.

As the days passed things became more intense with the career situation. I received further phone calls from the Smiling Assassin and others within the management team and they were all getting pushier and pushier about my return. It all started to become a bit of a blur since I was so high on morphine and by this time, not much mattered. I was starting to enjoy doing nothing, lying in bed pressing my bliss button for my hit of morphine or sneaking off with my morphine bag on a pole for a drug-induced cigarette and coffee in the stair well.

Finally, after seven days the doctors and specialists had worked out a plan for how to stick my arm back on and rebuild my elbow. At the time I had no idea what day it was or what the plan was and I could not have given a shit, I just wanted more morphine and a lie down and maybe a few more cigarettes and a coffee.

The plan was to insert three plates and forty-plus screws into my arm and piece back my elbow joint. (I'm told the elbow is one thing if damaged will grow back; good to know in my case). It was going to be a lengthy operation with no guarantees, all a little experimental and I was going to end up with some kind of bionic arm. I became well known on the ward only by my X-rays. Nurses and doctors would ask what was I in for and I would show them my arm and the common response was, "Ohhh you're that guy!"

The good news was the operation was a success and my arm was now stuck back on. About six hours after the operation I thought I would call a friend and have a quick cigarette just outside my room on the seventh-floor balcony. I was feeling damn good, still off my head-on morphine and the after-effects of the anesthetic, so I thought all would be fine. Sitting outside enjoying the late afternoon sun (or it may have been the morning, in my state I had no idea frankly), cigarette in hand and chatting away with my friend, out of nowhere… vomit attack!

I dropped my cigarette and phone on the ground and managed to violently projectile vomit green shit off the seventh-floor balcony. God knows where it landed or on whom, it was like some freaky shit out of that Poltergeist movie. I'm not sure if I was more shocked at the Poltergeist green vomit or that I had just vomited off the seventh floor of a hospital.

I managed to stumble to the bathroom and clean myself up, had a quick look in the mirror and I looked like total shit. I was a nice shade of green and my bloodshot eyes were kind of hanging out of my head. I knew something was not right and made my way back to my room as quickly as I could. Laying on my bed it all started again. Vomit attack, part two! No bullshit… I projectile vomited about three meters across the room hitting the wall on the other side. *Ow my lord… I am the poltergeist!* I thought.

I was now in a flat spin not knowing what the hell was going on, sweating like a madman, vomiting green shit everywhere and totally freaking out. Thank god for my roommate, she was screaming for help. Finally, the nurses came running in to help me. This was just the start to a truly messed up twenty-four hours of my life.

The next morning I woke up in intense pain. As I was madly pressing my bliss button for a good-morning hit of morphine. I noticed my arm had swollen and it was leaking fluid from every pore, kind of like sweating but more intense. I buzzed the nurse station once and waited five minutes. I buzzed again and still no nurse. My bliss-hit was starting to take effect as right before my eyes and my arm was getting bigger by the minute. I remember looking at my arm and having a little chuckle to myself, it looked enormous and my fingers were fat as sausages. Finally, a nurse turned up, took one quick look at my arm, poked it, looked at me in horror and ran off.

Next thing I knew I was surrounded by doctors, nurses and some specialist guy, all of whom were poking and prodding my sweaty arm. They all looked a little concerned but I was with the fairies in la-la land. They could have poked me in the eye and I still would have enjoyed it. Then it got all serious with the specialist asking far too many questions of me and two nurses started pumping me full of more drugs. I had no concept of what the hell was going on, I was just taking it all in and watching my arm and fingers slowly getting bigger and bigger as four to five large clean blisters started forming.

In all the drama I noticed my mother had arrived for a visit and the specialist guy was trying to explain to her what was going on with me. Looking up at my poor mother's face as I lay there drugged up, I could see in her eyes total disbelief and horror from whatever the specialist guy was explaining. It turned out I had had a severe reaction to the operation and my body was basically rejecting my new bionic-arm.

I found out weeks later I had a very small window of time between my body accepting my new bionic arm or having my arm cut off to safe my life. Something to do with my body going into distress, then into cardiac arrest and finally death. There I was again staring death in the face but this time I was completely oblivious to it, as well as the possibility that I was going to have my right arm amputated too! They say ignorance is bliss – guess they were right this time, because if I had known what was going I would surely have had a cardiac arrest.

This situation went on for what seemed like most of the week, with nurses in my face every few minutes, asking questions, poking my arm, squeezing my fingers and topping up my drug intake. I was still none the wiser to what was going on, and I just kept on pressing that little button for more bliss and looking at my fat fingers and having a giggle. Finally, my new bionic-arm started to return to its normal size. The only downside was I had massive fracture blisters that needed to have the tops cut off, drained and dressed.

Hospital life started to return back to normal, well as normal as it could be. In a twenty-four-hour period I had had a massive operation, got a bionic-arm, projectile vomited off of a seventh-floor building, faced death and come very close to losing an arm. So, all in all it was a mighty achievement. And, the good thing was I had my arm firmly attached. I think losing a leg would be ok, if you had a choice about losing a limb but just the thought of losing my right arm freaks me out. I am so very grateful to the people who saved it.

A few days later I had a visit from the specialist guy and surgeon to have a final debrief before returning home. Basically, they said I was one of the luckiest guys alive. The operation was a great success (apart from the "we might have to cut off your arm or you might die" part) and they thought I should get back about sixty to seventy percent use of my arm with intensive physiotherapy.

The funny thing was, I was getting quite used to all the attention in hospital, lying around getting hits of morphine every hour, watching TV and being fed three or four times a day. It was a much-needed break from the climb to my desired status to which I held onto so tightly too and all the bullshit of the corporate world.

ЖЖЖ

C H A P T E R   2 0 :
HOMECOMING AND RECOVERY.

After leaving home two weeks earlier to party with my friends, I was finally back. I could never have imagined that shit going down in a million years. Two weeks to get home from a party! (I once did two days). I guess you never know with life what is just around the corner. The good thing was, I was still alive, a little more screwed up mentally and physically but back in my own space to recover and finally back in my own bed.

Mum had dropped me home and we had take-out dinner together, chatted about the coming weeks of recovery, my career and how the hell I was going to cope by myself. Plus, I had to get the blister dressing changed every day with the high chance of infection. The coming weeks would be somewhat challenging.

The bionic-arm was not so bionic at this stage, still strapped to me in a sling but I so thought all would be fine and recovery should be easy. Yet again how little did I know! Career-wise, I had no idea what was going to happen; two weeks in business is like a lifetime and so much can change even overnight. I was feeling very anxious about going back to corporate-land. It would have been great to have more time to relax with some more morphine pumping through my body.

Once Mum had left I went upstairs and sat on my bed just for a moment and took stock. I was home, safe, yet all alone for the first time in two weeks. That's when the whole gravity of what had happened hit me. It was one weighty, overwhelming "what-the-fuck" moment of my life. I slowly leaned back and flopped onto my bed, lying there staring up at the ceiling when all my emotions just spewed out of every cell. I basically cried myself a river or a lake that night. Not very corporate-man of me but I think even corporate people cry sometimes.

I had been to hell and back in a two-week period, some of the things I experienced and saw in hospital stopped me in my tracks. Images of teenagers paralyzed from the neck down from a simple fall like mine, stuck in my mind. Just the thought of, *that could have been me,* scared the shit out of me yet; with my fall I got away with just a smashed arm. Hospitals are such morbid places, but I was so grateful to have walked out under my own power and not have been pushed out in a wheelchair. *Why was I lucky enough to walk away?* I still ponder that.

The experience also scared me deeply, the biggest thing was the fact it did happen to me. You read in the papers or see on TV this stuff happening to others: a freak turn of events that no one saw coming and then you find yourself living it. I was part of it and only just got away with it all and survived. Was I actually turning into Cat-man, complete with nine lives, or what? It was mind-boggling why life was presenting me with these experiences time and time again.

The thing I did come to realize over time was that life could change within a heartbeat, with no warning and really with no choice. The lesson was; it's not what happens to you in life, it's what you do about it that truly counts. The other things I learnt: I was so human, so vulnerable. I could be snuffed out at any second and I had zero control over it. Being a control freak (as I was) was a complete lost cause too; I had little control over so many things in life, yet the comforting thing was I had some great people around me and looking out for me.

One of those people was my sister. She had come back home from Samoa to look after me, drive me to appointments, change my blister dressing and generally help me out for a few weeks till I got back on my feet. Doing normal day-to-day things were a little problematic, like trying to get dressed, food shopping or trying to wipe my ass... the simple things in life. I was still taking pain relief and loving it, although becoming more and more dependent emotionally on the drugs to get through the day. The great thing was, it numbed the physical and also the emotional pain somewhat, which was brilliant!

Physiotherapy started a week after getting out of the hospital and I was going two to three times a week. It seemed like such an uphill battle and so damn painful trying to stretch out and use my new bionic-arm. I knew the process all too well – I had been down that path before when I broke my back. That had been a twelve-month recovery, plus learning how to walk again. At only eighteen then I had that fight for life thing going on but, being thirty-seven and fast approaching a mid-life-crisis or some type of spiritual-life awakening thing, I was very much lacking a teenager's fighting spirit. Still I pushed on.

My corporate life was calling me and it was time to re-enter on a part-time basis, which really pissed off management. They were expecting me back full time and all guns blazing. Day one in corporate-land and all had changed, and it proved another 'what the fuck' moment! While I was in the hospital the Smiling Assassin had hired more new sales staff who had no frickin' idea what they were doing. I would be solely responsible for managing and training these additional people plus the current people and still hit sales targets. It was as though I was given a teaspoon and told to dig a hole to China.

Sitting in my office I starting to wish I was back in hospital being pumped full of morphine again, relaxing, watching TV and buzzing off my head. Well they say be careful what you wish for. A week later I was back in the hospital, when my recovery came to an abrupt halt along with my digging a hole to China.

In the rebuild of my elbow and upper arm, the doctor had to saw off my forearm and then re-attach it with a mental plate and screws. In doing so, the doctor got the placement wrong, my forearm curving off to the right by two inches. Plus, one of the main screws in my elbow joint was too long and scraping the shit out of the joint.

There was some good news that week though. My brand-new sports car had arrived and it was the start of an intense materialistic love affair. She was a beautiful piece of engineering, shining, sleek, black and purred like a kitten… I was so in love! Surprising what a hunk of metal can do for you, and I was very happy. She would finish off my outward materialistic appearance perfectly. I had it all now! The career status, money, loft apartment, expensive clothes and now the wheels to get me around in style. There was only one setback, the bionic-arm had to be rebuilt and I couldn't drive for several weeks, all a bit torturous really!

So, it was off with my arm again and back on the morphine train to bliss-ville. I was in hospital for another four days, clearly management was not happy but the operation was a success... Well so everyone thought so at the time. Yet again, how little did I know what I was in for with my new and somewhat dodgy bionic-arm in the coming months.

It was back to recovering and to square one with physiotherapy. I was so pissed off; it was quite a defeating feeling starting all over again. I just wanted the whole thing to be done with and to have a normal life without doctors, specialists, physio and the pain! Not to mention all the medication I was on, which just screwed with my head.

And then there was the bullshit from corporate-land to top all it off! I remembering thinking there has to be a better life out there somewhere for me. I dug deep to gain some positive momentum in my life and pushed forward in the hope things would get better.

Ж Ж Ж

THE SETBACKS CONTINUE.

Life was getting pretty much back to normal, and I was back into my career full time, the dodgy bionic-arm was coming along, and things in general were starting to look better. After several hard weeks of physiotherapy and a lot of painful work I had managed to get back about eighty-five percent use, which was a frickin' miracle, considering the amount of damage I had done.

Career-wise I thought all was good, working long hours and starting to make headway with new and old staff and of course the management team. In the back of my head I was still bugged by the thought I needed to get the hell out of corporate-land and find something that would really support and satisfy me, my life and of course my health.

I was still meeting with Guru-Guy once or twice a week and talking more and more about me, the core problems, what made me tick and what was very important to me and my life. I guess in a way I was doing a spiritual apprenticeship with Guru-Guy, he was my master and I was the grasshopper, so to speak – very 'Karate Kid'. The more I read and the more I listened, the more I started to realize that my days were numbered with my toxic lifestyle and deluded sense of status. In some ways, in fact in many ways, this scared the shit out of me. It was me – my identity. If I gave it all up or turned my back on everything I had worked so damn hard for, who the hell would I be?

I could feel deep within me the changes starting. The idea of being and having everything began to lose its value slowly over time. The fight to sustain having everything and continue being something I was not, was a fierce battle of my competing minds. The universe or life situations were going to guide me in a very different path but I had some further lessons to be shown, some good and some horrifying.

First up was an ego blow of some magnitude. It started with a call from the Smiling Assassin requesting a meeting. It was around midmorning and I went off to meet him, with coffee, notepad and pen in hand. I walked into his office to find most of the management team sitting there all looking at me as though something horrible had happened or was about to. The feeling in my guts was not a good one; I knew something not so good was about to be revealed and I was not going to be a happy man. The atmosphere was thick with tension; you could have cut the air with a knife.

Making things a little more interesting, I notice the newly appointed acting human resources manager was sitting in on the meeting too. To start with he was a great guy, or so I thought. Forty-something, ex-police force dog-squad, very easy to get on with, and I believed we were developing a solid working relationship and a fairly good honest friendship too. I did confide in him from time to time – the only thing was at times I could feel there was a lot more going on with him than met the eye and not in a good way. Dog-man, as I called him, was also a close family friend of the Smiling Assassin which made for an interesting dynamic within the management team.

The meeting got underway with the Smiling Assassin stating that he and the management team (basically him and more so my old friend the Bald-ego) thought it best for me to step down from the Sales Manager position.

I sat there staring at him in disbelief as I felt my career and status start to choke the life out of me. *What the heck was going? Why… why… why?* I started to get the cold-hot sweats as my head imploded at the gravity of what he just said started to sink in. The Smiling Assassin said they weren't too sure why they had come to the decision but it was final. He went on to say they wanted me to stay with the company but in my old position as part of the sales team.

Bald-Ego was sitting there with a smug expression on his face as if he had just won some sick egomaniacal battle, and was standing back surveying the fatalities. The whole situation made me feel sick to my stomach as I lowered my head staring at the floor, overcome with a weird feeling of having been betrayed. It felt like I had just found out that my spouse was having an affair with my best friend and I was going to lose everything that I thought was so dear to me.

I was married to my career; I had far too much of me invested in it. It was as though my job title was my child and it had just been run over by a reckless driver, right in front of my eyes. Then I had the humiliating thought of how I was going to face the sales team now that I had, in the eyes of management, failed. How the hell would I tell my family and friends that I had been demoted and no longer in management? My identity just had its arms ripped off and it was bleeding out.

Over the years I had given this company so much of myself, too much – sold my soul type of thing – and I was all too loyal to them. They had just screwed me over and hard. This was not the first time and in the near future I would find it was not to be the last either. Within days I was going to be delivered further crushing news and it would really undermine my trust of people and corporate-land. I guess the good news was I still had a job, money was coming in and I could just prop up my career in the hope things would get better. The other good thing that sprung to mind was, I no longer had to manage or baby-sit the Kid, nor the Coked-up Stalker – I could sit back and watch the circus continue.

Straight after the meeting Dog-Man grabbed me and we went for a smoke and coffee. He was very interested in how I felt about the situation, my thoughts and what my next move might be. Would I get the shits and leave or just step down and be a good boy? The thought of blowing up the offices did pass through my mind but I was honest with him. At the time I had no idea what my next move would be, my head was spinning and I just wanted to curl up and die.

He persisted with question after question to a point where I felt quite interrogated, although he was also very understanding and consoling. It was all a little confusing, but I still felt that he had my back and would support me moving forward. As I said before, I thought we were developing a solid working relationship, if not a trusted friendship. My gut was telling me something was up however, and I had a slight uncomfortable feeling that I was being ever so softly corporately molested.

The next day in the office another meeting was called with the Smiling Assassin, Bald-Ego and Dog-Man. The announcement was – and this is the kicker (or a kick in the teeth for me) – the Dog-Man would be the new Sales Manager with immediate effect. I was also expected to support him and show him how to run the sales team, KPIs, budgets, targets, processes and so on. There was a silent expectation from the three men looking at me that I would be a good boy and comply, as they sat there waiting for my response.

At that moment in time I felt corporately-gang-raped by the people I had given not only my loyalty to, but also most of my waking hours and even virtually sold my soul to them. It was beyond words! My corporate-land dream in my head came to a bone-rattling stop that day as I looked at these men in front of me. Sitting there I thought, *What the hell are you people doing? You have no idea how your actions have just crushed me on so many levels.* And they all just sat there looking back, dead in the eyes while they continued verbally vomiting out further bullshit and insisting how all was ok and it was for the best.

They had played me and played me well! In my crushed and deluded state, I thought I had one up on them. I knew their business inside out; I had written most of the processors and had solid relationships with most of the clients. If I walked out I would take a lot of the clients with me, plus years of knowledge and more importantly, their precious revenue. They knew this and I knew this, and I realized I was in a great position to re-negotiate a new salary package to tide me over to my next move. This kind of soothed my bashed ego and fed it too, because I could now boost my financial status and it would be great for my well being too, no more pressure of being in management.

One thing I found hard to take was Dog-Man's actions, it felt like he had got out his dog-gun and shot me fair in the back of the head. The whole time he was maneuvering and manipulating the situation – and me. The realization of this was gut-wrenching, I had been screwed over by someone I had thought had my back. My trust and faith in people were shattered and just the thought of having to work and support Dog-Man made my skin crawl.

The interesting thing was, I had witnessed what some people would do in corporate-land to improve their status. Some are happy to use others as a human step to get what they want, but was I part of that too? The whole situation ultimately was all part of a hard learning curve; I can look back now and see the universe guiding me, not so gently in the direction I needed to go. If only I could have seen that then and just flowed with it all and not taken it so personally, my life would have been a lot easier.

I knew I had to suck-it-up and move forward if I wanted to support my deluded lifestyle further and that's what I tried to do, regardless of the outcome. If only I was more aware then of what I know now. I was deeply stuck in my head. I remember thinking how life was so, so cruel and unfair. The more I thought this, the more I experienced it and the following months would truly test my ability to face adversity.

ЖЖЖ

CHAPTER 22:
AND THE LESSONS CONTINUED.

Back to my old way of life, no management duties, just sell-sell-sell at all cost! My bullshit career in crazy corporate-land was in full swing. I was focused on the next sale like a junkie starving for his next hit and pushing myself to put my management failure behind me. The humiliation seemed to follow me everywhere as I re-adjusted my status and newly styled identity. I dragged my sorry-ass around for months faking to everyone that I was happy and that this was for the best. I even started to believe my calling was to be a salesman, not management, and I could just sell-sell-sell stuff for the rest of my life. Yet that voice in the back of my head was telling me to get out.

I was still persisting with Guru-Guy and the self-help books, trying to stay focused on the "now" and dumping my past regrets. What haunted me the most was the thought of not having done enough for Kev while he was alive. It was with me day and night. Basically I was lost without him, or more to the point, lost without the purpose of looking out for him. I had no fucking idea what I was honestly doing with my life, but then does anyone truly know? My life looked nice and rosy on the outside to a bystander, however inside it was a different story – so much confusion and conflict. I was at war with myself and it was all about what I "should" do; living my life to appease the expectations of others, instead of what was best for me.

My attention was to be redirected when the dodgy bionic-arm had a major malfunction. As it turned out, when the surgeon went in for operation two, he left me with a nice little present: A nasty infection. The new mental plate used to attach my forearm was suspected to have not been cleaned properly. So, I ended up in the hospital emergency again and again and again for overnight stays with intravenous antibiotics.

This went on for a few months – in and out of the hospital, more specialist appointments and no real solution. I just hoped the infection would somehow magically disappear and this shit would stop. The worrying thing was if they opened me up again, there was an even higher risk of more infection getting into my body. The other opinion was that there was a higher risk the infection would get into the bone and then I would be truly screwed. Like facing death kind of screwed. It felt like a never-ending story!

The last time I ended up in the hospital emergency room I was feeling less than well, the infection had taken hold of me and I knew things were not good. Yet trying to be positive, I drove myself to hospital hoping it would be a few hours of I-V antibiotics. How little did I know...?

Once there the nurses fussed around me doing their thing and then it all got so surreal. I don't remember too much but what I do remember is people started freaking out around me jabbing me with needles and sticking things on my body. Then I found myself in a bed with tubes hanging out of both arms this time and I was hooked up to machines going blip every few seconds.

The infection had spread throughout my whole body stressing out my heart, which was slowly coming to a stop and my blood pressure had dropped dangerously low. Lying there rather perplexed about the whole situation and wondering if it was really happening, I thought, *what the fuck is going on with my world?* Was I about to use up another cat-man life?

Perhaps the answer to that was yes because after a few hours they managed to stabilize me and moved me to a ward for further tests.

The decision was made to operate and remove the plate as soon as possible, so it was back to the operating table for me. This also meant it was back to square one with recovery and physiotherapy, plus more time away from corporate-land. Be that good or bad, this time it was a little different: I had multiple deals going on with new and old clients and the pressure was on to close… close… close! And you can't close deals while lying in hospital off your head on morphine. So, I had the not-so-pleasant phone calls from the Smiling Assassin and also Dog-man wanting to know what the hell was going on and when I would be back in the office to close the deals.

Lesson learnt from the previous time in hospital, I basically agreed with everything they said and just went with the flow. I could only do so much from the hospital and dosed up on morphine, and I was in no state to be closing deals…Yet they kept on calling! I started to realize that just maybe they needed me more than I needed my career and this thought was like a small seed that would grow with confidence over time. Life gave me a split second within this shitty situation to see my inner truth and worth, as it gently started to guide me onto a new path.

ЖЖЖ

LESSONS LEARNT: #7

"The more I learn,
the less I realize I know."

C H A P T E R 2 3 :
HEADING TOWARDS A NEW PATH.

Over the following months and into 2009 it was head down, bum up and work, work, work. Corporate-land was chugging along ok, still with the same endless bullshit and games by all involved however. The dodgy bionic-arm was coming good but only after some intense physiotherapy and a shitload of pain. My state of mind was somewhat stable for a change, clearly the Guru-Guy, the books and upping my meds was working plus I had started meditating most days. The corporate hippy within was slowly but surely metamorphosing, and it felt like I was heading down the right path.

The year of 2009 was an interesting one on many fronts; it was the calm before the storm. The coming year was going to screw me in the head from every which way and I would lose so much that was dear to me, yet gain further insight into life on this planet. However, within the calmness of 2009 I learnt a whole lot more about myself, about life and others around me – lessons that would at times show me who I could be.

With my life looking perfect from the outside, I continued to feed my delusions with money and mundane materialistic crap. Still I was getting more and more interested in the hippy-shit side of things, and I began to contemplate the question – isn't there more to life? So, on my quest for more knowledge and trying to work out if there really was more, corporate-land sprung a surprise on me. The Smiling Assassin made a bold move and got in a business/personal coach guy for the sales staff to assist in getting better results.

And so arrived the Coach-Guy. He was a frickin' genius. In his late fifties, he had done it all in business, travelled the world, experienced life's ups and downs, and was super positive and a genuine man. I had an instant connection with him, he got me and I totally got him. He became a very important mentor in my life. It was amazing how one person in your life could make such a major impact. He inspired me to be more honest with myself and look hard at my career and ask those scary-as-shit questions like, what do I truly want?

So now I was getting hippy-with-it in corporate-land too! I'm sure Coach-Guy would have been "on it" in the sixties: drugs, parties, sex and rock 'n' roll. It was such a refreshing break from the others and their bullshit games. Coach-Guy changed my view of myself and the corporate landscape in which I spent most of my time. Well just a little, I still had all my negative bullshit stories going on in my head. The corporate-gang-rape thing was still fresh in my mind, plus Dog-Man "shooting" me in the back of the head. Understandably I had developed some very unhealthy trust issues with anything corporate.

While that was all going on, I managed a short holiday to visit my sister in Samoa. What an amazing country and culture. The scenery was epic, like something out of Jurassic Park and the beaches were a pure slice of heaven. I was very fortunate to stay a few nights at

Lalomanu, right on the white sandy beach; it was just what I needed.

Having time to hang out with my sister, swim, get some sun and reflect on my newfound love, or at least "like" for life, made me realize many things. Guru-Guy and Coach-Guy had opened my mind up and guided me towards a different way of thinking and seeing life. I was feeling damn good about things and just being in a different country lying on a beach with no pressures made me feel incredibly hopeful that I could indeed change my life for the better, although I would need a push to get the ball rolling.

Before I knew it, I was back in corporate-land, holiday over and it sucked. I just felt like holidaying more or even packing up my shit and taking off to travel the world. Travelling to Samoa and seeing a different way of life kind of answered that question, "Isn't there more to life?" This got me thinking, maybe experiencing different countries and cultures would be the answer. The seed was planted, I knew one day I would just crack and say fuck-it to my deluded lifestyle, corporate-land bullshit, the money and walk away from it all. Just that brief thought warmed my soul and brought a smile to my face, it felt for a moment like I was truly alive! I think I started to see a very small and faint light at the end of the tunnel... Was it hope?

Those feelings didn't last too long. I couldn't go anywhere as I had some inner weird-assed responsibility to stay put and keep looking after my ever-so-slowly dying mother who was riddled with cancer. I think I made her my replacement purpose for Kev and if I focused on helping and supporting her, I could avoid, to an extent, facing up to my own shit further. Don't get me wrong, I loved her very much.

We had a very volatile yet honest relationship and I would have done anything for her. That "doing anything" for her would be tested in the near future, much to my surprise and I would go beyond what I thought I was capable of with wholehearted compassion.

ЖЖЖ

CHAPTER 24:
SOME CALM BEFORE THE STORM.

And so it looked as though the pre-tempestuous 2009 would end that way. I was working hard, studying and renovating my apartment, and had some time-out to reflect without any major dramas or nasty mishaps for me and for that, I was so very grateful. The previous two or so years had taken their toll on me mentally, physically and spiritually. In a weird way, through all the bullshit, pain and grief I was becoming a better person or at the very least, more understanding about life, others and myself.

However, my mind was still wandering off to paranoid thoughts. *All is going too well,* I said to myself, something is going to go wrong soon. These ran around my head continuously as though I was a crazed man. I guess I always got a little nervous when my life was operating smoothly and then *boom!* Someone loses an eye or almost an arm in my case. Yet I tried to stay focused on all the good things I had experienced, or obtained: I was living a dream I desired so much and had it all.

There was one eye-opening moment late in 2009, getting text messages from friends about my sister saying they hoped she was ok. At first I had no idea what the hell was going on until I got a phone call from my mother (as you can imagine I was starting to get somewhat freaked out when she called unexpectedly) telling me that there had been a massive earthquake in Samoa and a suspected tsunami was going to hit the island.

Mum was all but in tears and I sat there a little stunned for a moment and then thought, *Noooooooo! Not my sister and nephew! This can't be frickin' happening.*

I was very close to my sister and just the thought of her being killed filled me with utter panic and despair. It was one of the longest days of my life, and finally after hours of waiting, we heard from her. She was safe, although shaken up. My sister is one of those special people you meet in life, the ones that rise to the top in a drama or time of need and get shit sorted. She managed to help and support many people while she was in Samoa, especially after the tsunami hit. Her stories of the aftermath still chill me to my bones.

The tsunami hit Samoa around nine a.m., killing many people and totally obliterating the slice of heaven Lalomanu where I had stayed only months before. It was heartbreaking to know that the beautiful people I had met on my travels, the people I had met while I relaxing and reflecting on my life, were more than likely all dead. Truly a very sad day for Samoa. The whole situation did get me thinking once more… Is *life all about timing?*

My sister, nephew and mother were in Lalomanu just days before. I was just so, so, so grateful they were all safe. I was not sure how I could have dealt with losing another family member. But, how little did I know, within months I would have to face up to that bitter reality.

With life speeding forward regardless of death or disasters, Christmas and a new year were just around the corner. The lead up to Christmas was very special; most of my family including me were planning a good old country Christmas on my cousin's farm. Plus, the fact that I would be having a break away from the bullshit of corporate-land and of course getting some good country cooking and fresh air, which meant that life was looking good!

The final months of 2009 were great. My sister had returned from Samoa something of a changed woman and with her son in tow, we were off to Bali for a week. Bali is such a special place for me: the culture, the people, and the energy. It seems to ground and energize me all at the same time. The other thing is that Bali is the place where as a family we let go of Kev… On a physical level. We had all gathered on the main beach at sunset with Kev's ashes and we sprinkled his remains into the ocean as the sun slowly set in the distance.

There was a massive "ooow arrrr" moment though. Just after we had finished sprinkling his ashes, the clouds with those rich red and orange highlights starting forming into the shape of Kev's face.

We all stood there staring into the sky in total amazement, the feeling in my chest, I guess my heart, was one of warmth that he was still with us all yet in some other form or dimension. It was truly a moving moment in time and one that I will never forget.

So, finishing off the year with a trip to Bali and also all the support and guidance from Guru-Guy and Coach-Guy, I honestly felt I was travelling in the right direction, at least with my hippy-life. In terms of my career and corporate-land, I was not so sure.

One thing I was sure about: I was feeling so damn grateful for 2009 and for those people coming into my life just when I needed them. The old laws of attraction were working in my favor. It still surprises me that when I did get calm and think of what I truly needed in my life and then imagined I had it, it would just appear! However, that goes for the bad shit too and I learned that the hard way and to an extent I still slip up on, from time to time.

ЖЖЖ

CHAPTER 25:
THE LAST CHRISTMAS.

While I was in Bali my mother thought it would be a great idea to break her leg, of course by accident, not sure how she did it, something to do with getting the mail from the mailbox and then falling in the garden… As you do! Anyways it was a blow to her health considering she was still trying to fight her never-ending cancer battle.

My mother hated her cancer with an incredible passion. The way I see it, cancer is a case of our own cells going bad. So, in a spiritual or hippy way of thinking you are fighting yourself essentially, solely focused on the battle and not on good health. In these terms she was basically hating herself to death.

I am more aware now that when you hate a part of yourself with that much passion you only get sicker and if you can love yourself unconditionally with acceptance of whatever illness you have, that's where the magic happens and you heal. I guess what I am trying to say is, the more you focus on something, the more of it you get.

I visited my mother once I got back from Bali, I think it was the first night, just to check up on her and make sure she had everything she needed. Sitting there with her I could feel in my stomach and see in her eyes things were not good. It was one of those feelings again, not a thought just a slight uncomfortable feeling, like a sixth sense that all is not well and that the shit will hit the fan in the near future.

We chatted for a while about general stuff and our trip to the farm for Christmas and how she would get there and back. My mother was a stubborn and tough lady; she was determined to drive herself complete with broken leg plus her latest foster child. After a while, my sister and I managed to convince her to fly and we would sort out drop offs and pickups.

And so Christmas was upon us and it was time to head off to the farm. I was in my car and all alone which was great! I love a road trip: fresh air, open highways and… Space! Finally, I could get out of the city with my materialistic love affair, my black sleek sports car. Damn she was great, I had raced cars when I was younger and had developed quite an addiction for speed; there was nothing better… Hmmm, well maybe morphine. That day I was getting a massive dose of it, with insane speeds as I blasted through the countryside.

Christmas was a special time for me with family and friends yet this year was so different. It was the third year without Kev and in the back of my mind I was thinking that it might be the last Christmas with my mother too. That really did freak me out yet I thought it was best to make the most of it and so I did. I wanted to give my mother something from the heart and something that would assist her or give her some type of peace of mind in her cancer battle. I couldn't help but feel her days were numbered and it was important to me that she knew it, I guess on a higher level if not a little hippy, I wanted to help her on her pending transition.

I had just read a book by Mitch Albom, *Tuesdays with Morrie*. It was such a touching and honest story. It was about two good friends – a student and his former professor. The professor was slowly dying from a terminal illness, so the student spent every Tuesday with the professor and wrote about the process and the lessons learnt. It touched me deeply and I related to it in some strange way. It reminded me very much of my situation with my mother. So, I gave my mother this book for Christmas in the hope she would read it and somehow feel comfortable or even peaceful about her own terminal illness.

I just wanted to do something, anything to change the situation. It is such a head-fuck to see not only someone you love, but the person that gave birth to you, suffer and suffer for so long. At least I thought this book might bring some peace to her thoughts.

When she opened my gift on Christmas morning she stared at the book cover for just a moment with acknowledgement, as I looked on nervously. To be honest I was not sure how she would react, talking about death or even taking it seriously in my family was somewhat difficult. Then my mother slowly raised her head looking me straight in the eyes and with a little smile on her face, and said lovingly, "Thank you love".

In those few seconds of eye contact, it felt like we both conceded to the fact her time was near. It was such a small exchange; there were no words, just a very subtle o.k. I see now what you see within me. That moment will stick in my head for the rest of my life.

We all stayed on the farm for a few more days after Christmas and pretty much just drank, ate and laughed a lot. It was one of the great Christmases to remember. I still hold on tight to those memories to this day yet the thought of Christmas these days with neither mother nor little brother breaks my heart. It freaks the hell out of me that life just keeps rolling on regardless of what has happened, what will happen and what's happening right now!

ЖЖЖ

CHAPTER 26:
GO, GO, GO... 2010.

B ack into the real world: corporate-land, career and making money. No fresh air nor open spaces, it was full steam ahead through the concrete jungle and bullshit. I had decided 2010 was going to be "my year". I was going to finish my studies and renovation, make some serious money and basically just have a great year. I was pumped up about a new year and new opportunities. Yet again, how little did I know what the hell was about to unfold. I was in for one all-encompassing ride to hell and back, then back to hell and then spat out into a new reality. I sit here writing this and I'm staggered to believe I am still alive and relatively sane. Ok... so I'm not that sane... I'm living breathing proof of "work in progress".

It was around day sixteen of the New Year and bam! My year had suffered a major derailment which would proceed into a total train wreck in time. I was sick and I mean extremely sick. This was so not the plan and I was pissed off. I had no idea what the hell was wrong with me but I knew it was not good. Again, I had that weird stomach-churning feeling that I was in for a nasty ride and a nasty ride it would be.

In the third week of "my year" I was sitting in the Doc-B's offices waiting to see him. Doc-B ran every test he could with all his gadgets which showed some signs of what was wrong, and then I was off to get further tests, blood tests, scans and any other test he could think of. From what I did sense, Doc-B was rather concerned with my health status which did nothing for my wellbeing or paranoia. All I could think was, *What the hell is wrong with me? Am I dying or what?* I had to wait a week or so for the results of all the tests as I got sicker and sicker.

For those days, I just dragged my ass around in corporate-land from meetings to home and to my mother's place. I was like the walking dead, I don't remember too much of the details of what I actually did or who I saw, some days I couldn't even get out of bed. It's damn frightening when you're that sick and I remember thinking, *Can I still be alive and this sick?* It made me realize my health was very important – it was everything, for a good and happy life.

What if I was going to be sick forever?

This thought scared the shit out of me and then I started thinking about my cancer-fighting mother. Her health had been all over the place for ten years to the point where she was in and out of hospital many times and came within milliseconds of losing her life on one or two occasions due to, believe or not, doctors' total incompetence. How the hell did she cope mentally and emotionally all the time? And how did she deal with her doctors giving her notice that her health and life was pending? The doctors had given her four to six years back in 2001 and the old-girl was still kicking ten years later… Well just about, she was starting to fall apart literally and lose her mind.

Speaking about losing their minds, I was on that bus and needed some answers! Finally, Doc-B called to tell me my results were back, it was time for all to be revealed and I was shitting myself with fear. I remember turning up to his offices feeling like a bag of shit and worried out of my head about what was about to be uncovered. Sitting patiently in the waiting room as the time passed ever so slowly, it felt like torture. As always, Doc-B was running behind time with patients, which just gave me even more time to totally get into my head and think of all the possible freaky things I may have... *Do I have cancer? Maybe a brain tumor? Or HIV? Oh, wait; I would have had to have sex for HIV.* Sad story: no time for sex, I was too busy having marital problems and dealing with my bullshit career.

My thoughts hovered around the possibilities of cancer and that was one thing I would not wish on anyone! Watching my mother go through her intense battle with that bastard was breathtaking in a completing screwed up way. I was taking her to all her chemo, doctors and specialist appointments, so I witnessed firsthand what the cancer show was all about and I wanted no part of it! I had so many things going on in my head and then Doc-B's door opened and it was my time to enter and get some fairly life changing news.

I sat down and looked at Doc-B. He had his pity face on which meant the news was not going to be good. I settled myself, took a deep breath and nervously let the air drift out of my mouth before asking the question, "So Doc-B, what's wrong with me?" I was trying so hard to be positive yet, I had voices in my head shouting out, "You got cancer – you got cancer."

Doc-B looked back at me with a more intense pity and tilted his head to the right slightly and said, "Well the news is not good Tim, I'm sorry to say, the test results indicate you have lymphoma but, we will need to carry out further tests to be 100% sure you have cancer". I think at that point, my mind, thoughts and body just… flat-lined! *Holy shit.* "I have cancer" was repeating itself in my head over and over again, getting louder with every repetition. I sat there totally still, as if frozen in time. Slowly I broke into a cold sweat. My whole life flashed before my eyes as my expectations for my future fell out of the sky like dead birds mid-flight.

Looking back at my Doc-B visit, I remember thinking, "You're so full of shit and you have no idea what you are talking about." I was off to the land of denial, my family's favorite holiday destination when confronted with bad news. Whilst in this no man's land my grandmother came to mind, who had been taken in the nineties by the very same cancer I was potentially facing. And with that I sprang back into reality.

I went on to ask every conceivable question about lymphoma and what I had to do next. Doc-B informed me that I would have to go to the cancer ward at the nearby hospital for further tests and he added that I would be a very lucky man if it were not lymphoma. I wasn't feeling very lucky at all; my new year had just gone to hell. "What the fuck was I going to do if I had cancer?" That question was playing on auto repeat in my mind.

I couldn't help but feel I had been so happy and free, at peace no less, sitting in a field with the sun shining brightly and then out of nowhere the hand of God had smacked me into a really shitty place. I had worked so damn hard to get my life back on track and was starting to be in my "happy space"; I had everything I ever wanted and my life felt like it was on the right path. So much crap was madly running through my head as I sat in Doc-B's office while he was writing out referrals, banging away on his computer and making phone calls to different cancer professionals to help me.

I left Doc-B's offices a crushed man, feeling like total shit and full of despair. I sat in my car and rang my sister to let her know the new family news but no answer, so I called a good friend and no answer; I tried another friend and no answer. So, I just sat there in my fancy car, my designer suit and lit a cigarette. Words are not enough to describe the anguish I felt, but imagine having every tiny piece of hope sucked out of your soul and absolutely no one to empathize with you, and you will begin to get some idea of where I was.

Ж Ж Ж

CHAPTER 27:

HOSPITALS AND DOCTORS.

It was about thirty days into "my year" and everything was unraveling quicker than I could keep up with – not the start I was hoping for at all. I was trying very hard to stay positive and think happy thoughts… *Things would have to get better at some point,* I thought. In hindsight, I could not have been more wrong! Things were just warming up and coming to the boil; I was in for an extraordinary and involuntary jaunt into the cruel world of cancer.

I had informed the people that needed to know about my new situation: some family, corporate-land people and friends, but I kept it to a minimum. I was still very much of the mindset that once you started talking to others about your problems, that's when they grow legs and start taking over your life. I was still dragging around that half-dead horse and did not want to add to it. I was trying to downplay the whole situation, more than aware that if I thought about the cancer thing too much I would attract it into my life all the more. There was no need for me to get into a cancer battle, I had no time for that, I was too busy helping out in my mother's battle and that was enough for me.

One thing I didn't do was to tell my mother about my pending cancer tests, she was almost literally in the trenches fighting her own battle, still standing, but not for long. The situation in the coming days was more than a little ironic; it was borderline fucked-up. Either way it was defiantly confronting. My first round of tests was at one cancer clinic while on the other side of town in another cancer clinic my mother was starting her last-ditch attempt at chemo. This was all to be happening on the same day, in real-time and once I had finished my tests, I had to race across town and pick her up after her treatment.

Testing day had arrived. I had decided to go it alone. I didn't want someone with me asking me dumb-assed questions... "Are you ok? How do you feel?" I wanted to stay in the land of denial. I walked anxiously into the hospital to find the cancer clinic and I was overwhelmed by the very familiar smell you get in those places. It brought back so many memories of visiting my mother and of watching my father basically waste away over time when I was a teenager. It was a massive reality check and I was super paranoid that I might be ending up down that same road. It certainly gets you thinking about your own mortality!

Looking for directions to the cancer clinic I just wanted to run, this was the last place on earth I wanted to be in. I forced myself to stay focused on finding where I needed to go and get the bloody tests done and get the hell out of there. I kind of expected the cancer clinic to be just a reception/waiting room and a few consolation rooms... Another misguided expectation!

After about ten minutes of wandering around, I finally found the cancer clinic and walked into what looked like a standard waiting room and true enough it had a few hallways leading to, I guessed, the consolation rooms. I could hear the faint sound of medical equipment whirring away in the distance. I looked around and much to my surprise, at the end of one of the hallways, there were people sitting in big comfortable brown chairs with tubes hanging out of their arms.

I stood in the middle of the waiting room, somewhat in shock, staring at these people fighting for their lives, as machines pumped them full of little cancer-fighting soldiers to take up their battle. It was such a sobering sight and sadly a familiar one, as I had witnessed it many times over the years with my mother. But this time it was far too real. My heart was thumping so hard with the anxiety of what could become of me in the very near future.

I met with the cancer doctor or specialist, I wasn't really sure what she was at that point but she was very nice and understanding for the most part. We chatted for a while about my situation, running through every possible health-related question you could think of. I think I must have asked her a hundred times in different ways if she thought I had cancer. I just wanted to know, I didn't want to wait a second longer, I wanted answers and I wanted them there and then god-damn-it! I could sense she was getting more and more irritated with me as the process went on.

Finishing up she handed me a list of tests I had to have done: blood tests and other scans. Once I had completed all the tests it would take roughly another two weeks for the results to be ready. This made my blood boil with a mixture of emotions: anger being the clear leader closely followed by sheer anxiety with paranoia sprinkled on top. I slumped into the chair with the realization that this was going to be a long-drawn-out process, and I would have to just suck it up and get on with my life as best I could.

So, I left the cancer clinic none the wiser about what the hell was going on with me and the cancer thing hung heavy on my shoulders, nestling close to the half-dead horse. The feeling of being so damn helpless and having no real control was overwhelming as I drove across town to meet my mother. Thinking a lot as I drove, well completely over-thinking it really, I did at least manage to have a laugh, a somewhat nervous one, about the situation. There I was getting tested for cancer as my mother was being treated for it and fighting a very much losing battle.

What the fuck is going on with my life and how the hell did I get to this point?

Arriving to pick up my mother was like arriving at what was rapidly become a second family home: she had spent many months in this hospital and countless days in treatment there. This place with all its amazing doctors and nurses, and some not so amazing, had kept the old girl kicking along for close to ten years. Yet I hated the place, spending months on end there watching my mother suffer along with many others. It was so damn frightening that life could just turn on you at any given time.

Waiting in the cancer treatment area for her, I was starting to truly understand what my mother was experiencing with her battle. My battle was pending and it made the whole thing very real for me, especially after my trip to the cancer clinic that day. This also kicked off the whole "let's re-evaluate my life" thing and I had a moment of clarity about my life right there and then. If I was cancer-free and if my mother did eventually die, I would sell my materialistic crap, quit corporate-land and run, run, run from my deluded identity to some country or place far, far away.

Then I stopped and asked myself the question, "Can I do it, can I honestly do this?" From deep within and very loudly I got... "Hell yeah, you can do it!"

It was official, I had mentally, emotionally and frickin' spiritually cracked. Finally, it was time for change and I knew it. It scared the living hell out of me just thinking of it and I was sitting there shaking with fear and excitement all in the same moment. I then allowed myself to imagine what it would be like to run from my deluded and toxic way of life and I was filled with such a sense of relief and a feeling of endless freedom.

Smiling to myself I looked up to see my frail and slowly dying mother shuffle towards me. She was looking like total crap but still had a little welcome smile on her face for me. I gave her a big loving hug and a kiss on the cheek.

Driving her home the twenty questions started about my life started. It was, "What have you been doing?" and, "Why?" And, "What are you doing next?" And then she came out with it.

"What is wrong with you? You don't look well."

I guess all mothers know when something is up with their kids and she was onto me. My mother would have done well as an army interrogator or spy; she was always probing for answers about my life. I told her what was going on with my pending cancer battle and to this day, I can still hear her saying, "Oh no. Timothy, oh no!" The emotions within her words were of complete compassion and understanding for my situation; it warmed the soul of my inner child, like only a mother could.

Ж Ж Ж

CHAPTER 28:
NOT A PATIENT – PATIENT.

A few days later I was back at the hospital to get the second round of tests done… bloods, scans and whatnot. Needless to say, "my year" had officially gone to shit. With every passing day I was becoming more and more paranoid that it was cancer. I was really over-thinking the whole thing and only focused on the worst-case scenario which in turn was making me even sicker. I should have known better at the time yet, that old demon of mine had resurfaced. You know, the poor-me-and-why-is-this-happening-to-me one? Crap that most of us seem to entertain from time to time.

The old demon had planted firmly in my head the notion of an end-point-day. That imaginary day somewhere in the future when I would get the terrible news that I was so paranoid about hearing: that I had cancer and my life would be changed forever. The imaginary events were playing in my head like a YouTube clip on auto-repeat and I had no idea how to stop it. My hippy-shit was not helping me! In my head I had every possible response planned out and along with my very own pity party it was a 24/7 head-fuck. I just wanted it all to be all over. But there was a very small part of me loving the drama. I guess it was giving me some much-needed attention and care from others.

I was also making my life even more torturous with my "Type A" personality and all. I had little to no patience at the best of times and with no obvious light at the end of the cancer-testing tunnel. I was overloaded with study commitments and still in the final stages of my never-ending renovations. I was totally out of patience for any further crap. It was breaking point and I felt like a dead man in waiting.

While trying to keep myself together and resemble a functioning human, corporate-land was in my face again making even more demands on me and my time. Management wanted to squeeze out the last remaining drops of what was left of the soul I had sold them. I was now required to assist Dog-Man further in the operations of the sales team and somehow help him to be a sales manager.

My skin crawled at the mere thought of assisting this man; I couldn't forget him "corporately-shooting" me in the back of the head just months prior. In my eyes he had lost every fiber of the integrity I thought he had. Regardless of whether I was to help him or not, Dog-Man hadn't a hope in hell of getting his head around how to operate a sales team in the short term. He also had zero understanding of the cutthroat world of corporate IT and how to manage himself within that world. That was just one other thing I was meant to be helping him with.

With my sold-out soul, all but dried up, I just played along like a good corporate boy and tried to assist Dog-Man where I could. I didn't have the energy not to, but this time I was on high alert. It was like I was back in the DRC jungle on emergency survival mode. And it was the same in all aspects of my life; I had essentially regressed to cave-man survival mode.

Dog-Man continually used his acquired macho-bully police tactics as a way of managing people. Minus the dogs, of course, although I'm sure if he could have, he would have set his dogs on me and other colleagues. I really had to dig deep to deal with his macho-bully bullshit. I'm very much an anti-bully type of guy in any situation and I had experienced my fair share of it over the years in corporate-land. If only these corporate "men" could control their egos for a moment they might realize they would get a whole lot more with sugar than shit. And what a different world we would all be living in!

Speaking of egos, I also had my old friend the Bald-Ego watching my every move. The whole situation was like trying to manage two five-year-olds in a sandbox with only one tractor. The disheartening thing was they both knew of my cancer situation yet it was clear they didn't give a shit. They were too focused on their macho-bully management strategies to ensure targets were met, regardless of the personal lives of their colleagues.

Two things kind of saved me in the short term. First, my situation with the pending cancer test results. I was beginning to cultivate an attitude of not giving a shit what these men did or said. It was somewhat refreshing and new ground considering my tendency to want to control things and always put my point across. Secondly, finally some of the lessons and tools I had been learning were starting to sink into my thick head. I was beginning to achieve a feeling of total awareness of my thoughts and actions, and how it affected others. With this awareness, I was also becoming more passive and non-reactive with Dog-Man and Bald-Ego, and this seemed to confuse the hell out of them. I had basically stopped feeding their egos with my own ego crap and they began to back off.

These were very powerful tools to have in corporate-land. I used them a lot and it helped me to not get so personally involved in conflicts with them or others, by just observing instead. By being quiet and simply witnessing Dog-Man's macho-bully tactics, I learnt so much about manipulation and the egotistical mind in full swing. At times it was mind-boggling the lengths such men would go to just to be right. It was one massive step forward for me in that world and this gave me just the right amount of patience I needed not to massacre the entire office.

The small amount of patience I was able to scrape together at work didn't flow over into my personal life unfortunately. I was calling the doctor's office every day, sometimes three or four times, asking about my results. About ten days had passed and still no news either way, no callbacks from the cancer-clinic nor Doc-B. So, I just kept on calling and calling and calling them. I was starting to understand the life of a stalker: it's very time consuming and there's a lot of waiting around!

It was such a frustrating situation to be in. I was waiting for the words "Yes you have cancer" or "No, you don't". But this got me thinking even more! "If it was a no, when what the hell was wrong with me? And what was next?" If a yes, it would be a one-way ticket to the cancer show, sitting next to my mum.

The more time passed without knowing, the more intensely the looped You-Tube clip of imminent doomsday played in my head. It was driving me bloody crazy with anxiety, and the well-meaning persistence of caring friends and family asking me every day what was going on wasn't helping much either.

"Have you heard yet? Is it cancer? Are you ok?"

I know people were very worried but this just made it all too real, which freaked me out even further. I had no time for reality. I just wanted to crawl into bed and drift off to sleep in complete denial; so that I could wake up the next morning to find out it was all just a bad dream.

ЖЖЖ

CHAPTER 29:
IMAGINARY DOOMSDAY.

My imaginary day of doom had arrived and it was time for me to receive the devastating results. Well the ones I had conjured up in my head anyways. I remember getting the phone call two days earlier from the cancer clinic advising me my results were ready. Super-stressed and anxious, I demanded to know the results right there and then but the lady refused to give them to me over the phone. I felt like going totally frickin' mental at her as she calmly explained their policy and that I had to receive the results in person from the doctor herself.

In the split second after getting off the phone, my head exploded into a frenzy of utter anxiety. I lost complete control of my thoughts and was trying for the life of me to get my shit back together. It felt like I was sitting in a large vat of boiling toxic emotions with great big chunks of fear and panic bobbing around me as I stewed. I had pretty much convinced myself I had cancer and that was the only reason the lady wouldn't tell me my results over the phone.

I made my way back to the cancer clinic still feeling infuriated but as I reached my threshold of panic, it all collapsed into a kind of peaceful numbness. Whatever would be, would be, I thought. Maybe I was learning unconditional acceptance and was more hippy than I realized at the time.

Anyways, I finally got to see the Cancer-Doctor and she had all my results ready. She ushered me into a cramped, very bright room with a small desk and two chairs either side. It was like a frickin' FBI interrogation room you see on the movies. Somewhat off-putting, she sat there peering across the desk at me. I felt like screaming at her "What the hell is wrong with me lady?" I only just managed to control myself and take a few nervous breaths as she slowly opened my file, flicking through the papers. And then she paused.

The room was filled with unbearable silence; the type that is so heavy you feel like you're being crushed to death.

This is when I lost my peaceful hippy attitude and my head felt like it had burst into flames. My heart started thumping in time to a ticking clock on the wall.

Holy shit! Did I have cancer?

My whole being was focused on her next move as she ever so gracefully looked up at me with a half-smile.

"It's not cancer... It's not Lymphoma as expected." I must have been holding my breath because I let out the loudest sigh of relief and nearly blew the papers off her desk. I slumped back into the chair as a massive amount of adrenaline rushed through me.

I felt as if I'd stepped off the curb without looking and only by the grace of God had not been hit by a bus, instead just feeling the cool air rushed past my face. You know you are having a very lucky day in those moments and someone greater than you has your back.

The doctor then continued talking about the other test results. I had no idea what the hell she was saying, I was deep inside my own head reconciling the fact I didn't have cancer. By that point I had convinced myself I had it. I had played out a thousand times how I would react to the news and then how I would let everyone know. So, at the time I was feeling fairly confused on how to react and then the thought of, "Well… what the hell is wrong with me then?"

I think I must have screamed it at the doctor in the heat of the moment as well. She was glaring at me. She spoke firmly, "As I said before…" And went on to say I had the Epstein-Barr virus, or EBV for short, and some other secondary virus that would indicate I had Lymphoma, like a false-positive. EBV is pretty nasty anyway, but it was the second time I had had it. In conjunction with the secondary virus plus the fact that I was pushing forty, I was one very sick corporate-hippy.

She strongly suggested bed rest for as long as it took to get back to some normal state of existence. She was also very aware of my corporate-land commitments and the growing stresses, and was fairly clear that that world was a no-go zone for the near further. I was to have no stress of any kind.

I was being led to believe that having the two viruses at the same time at my age and with any further stress would do serious damage to my health. I sat there taking all the information on board. *What the hell was I going to do about my commitments with corporate-land?*

Basically, I chose to hear her say simply that I was slightly run-down and I needed to have a little nanny-nap, a cup of tea and everything would be fine in a few days. *How little did I know…?*

I so should have listened to her more seriously!

ЖЖЖ

LESSONS LEARNT: #8

"I have found over time facing my fears and walking through them is a much better way than holding onto them.

To hold on too tightly only stops me from flowing and moving forward in my life."

PART-TIME SURRENDER.

The Cancer-Doctor wanted me to see Doc-B for a treatment plan and I also needed to get further paperwork to prove to Dog-Man and the management team I was in fact sick. In corporate-land regardless of how sick you are, even if you were slumped over the photocopier dead for all to see, you need the paperwork to get paid for any time off. So, it was back to see Doc-B and find out what I needed to do to get better. And of course pick up the frickin' paperwork.

My visit was quite an eye opener and a very unexpected dose of reality was shoved down my throat. Doc-B knew my full medical and personal history, which included all my corporate-land dramas. He had in the past suggested I take time out from the stresses of my personal and corporate life and chill out on a beach for several months. I think he was starting to get sick of the sight of me.

However, this time he showed genuine compassion and empathy towards me. Just before he gave me some borderline violent tough love. Sitting at his desk with all his medical gadgets surrounding him, he lent forwards, looking me dead in the eyes.

"If I could climb over this desk and punch you in the face I would!"

He went on a rant telling me how sick, stressed and burnt out I was and if I didn't change my lifestyle and get out of corporate-land I would be a dead man at some point in the very near future!

I couldn't get a word in. It I felt like I was back at school in front of the principal being berated like a naughty little boy. I had no choice but to sit there and take it all. Some things I thought were total bullshit until my inner self-preserving voice stepped in. It gently whispered to me. 'You know he is right; you have to change your life.' This rattled around my head before I came to the dreaded realization: I had to change my life if I still wanted a life. In the past I had thoughts of walking away from corporate-land and imagined doing it but this was like a firm punch to the forehead. And it got my attention!

I remember sitting in Doc-B's office in shock. In my head my whole deluded lifestyle with its fancy apartment, sports car, money and corporate-land status started breaking apart like a doomed aircraft mid-flight. It rattled me so much that I was almost got on my hands and knees to surrender myself to the situation and change my life. The one thing that freaked me out the most was the clown-like voice running around in my head shouting, "How? How? How?"

How in God's name was I going to change my life?

I agreed with Doc-B to go on light duties in corporate-land with a view to planning a lengthy sabbatical to sit under a coconut tree and do nothing. I was only to work four to six hours per day and rest as much as possible. I also had to go back to seeing the Guru-Guy twice a week to talk about my stress issues and find a way to manage them better. The whole "how would I change my life?" thing was a confusing, yet surrendering to the situation I found myself in had a slight hint of empowerment to it, which gave me some peace.

My humbling experience with Doc-B had ever so slightly cracked my mind open to new possibilities, as scary as I thought they might be. My whole being and existence was under-pinned by what I had, what I did and what I thought I was: a corporate businessman. This was my identity, this was me! Well so I thought back then.

Half-lesson learnt, I left Doc-B's office and continued on with my deluded lifestyle, albeit at a much slower pace. In the back of my head I was hoping that with time I could overcome my illnesses, manage my stress levels better and again occupy my very important first-world-identity and feed my hungry egotistical mind.

But as time passed I was back into my old habits and the lesson was a mere speck in my past. Fear once again was the main driver in my life, of losing my precious identity and status, so I tightened my grip further on them both. It was as though I was holding the hand of a loved one so tightly while they dangled precariously on the edge of a cliff about to plunge to their death. The foolish thing was, that the harder I gripped on to my identity and status the more they slipped through my fingers; I was basically squeezing them both to death.

Life continued to push and shove me in vain attempts to make me see where I needed to go yet I kept on ignoring and resisting every suggestion. It's funny or insane maybe, because I did have some awareness of what was going on at the time, but for some reason I chose to side with my ever-so-important identity and status. Life sat back and observed me, but only for a short period of time though. It was preparing itself once again to truly teach me what I needed to learn and show me the essence of what it means to be a being human.

ЖЖЖ

FACING ACCEPTANCE.

Back in the corporate-land pit of bullshit and games, I was still fighting to keep my head above water whilst desperately trying not to commit any acts of career suicide. The pressure on me from Dog-Man, Bald-Ego and anyone else that thought they had some type of power over me was pushing me to my breaking point. I was still on light duties, much to the disgust of most of my colleagues. I tried to ignore it and with all the strength that I had, I focused on getting better regardless.

It was one of the hardest times I have ever experienced; just wanting to get on with my life only to slip slowly back into my old ways of complete, deluded madness. I was so willing, but not able, my body was screaming at me that enough was enough and then my spirit started to join in too. I tried to give myself some space to truly think about what the hell I was doing with my life, and more importantly, what I very much wanted. I spent a lot of time trying to reconcile myself with the thoughts of leaving corporate-land, dismantling my identity, status and recreating myself somehow, somewhere else.

An important and if not pivotal event took place within this time for me and showed me, finally, that my days in corporate-land were coming to an end.

I was working on a massive and complex deal with one of the largest not-for-profits (NFP) in Australia, trying to work out their software licensing compliance. Basically for every computer being used, it required a license key or code for the software. The NFP had received letters of demand from one of the world's leading-software-companies (LSC), stating that they were in fact not compliant. LSC had recently changed their licensing rules and now the NFP was in a very serious legal bind and was facing millions of dollars in order to become compliant. My task was to make the issue goes away as fast as possible ensuring complete compliance but with minimal dollars spent… It was game on!

The reason I was working with NFPs in the first place was all part of my corporate-hippy attitude, as a business man I believed that we didn't have to rape and pillage the whole town to make a dollar. Despite the corporate world I lived in, I wanted to make a difference and do the right thing in business terms for all involved. Perhaps naively, it just made me feel bloody good about myself that I could assist NFPs and get the right solution in place for them with only a minimal investment.

It was just doing the right thing "when no one was watching" and every time I did this, all parties were extremely happy with the outcome. The NFPs would at times save millions of dollars so then they could support their clients better, and these were people who needed it. The company I worked for got their cash and I got mine and it all felt a bit fairer without even a hint of raping or pillaging.

The whole theory was not rocket science it was just doing good old-fashioned business with a bit of integrity, when a handshake was of some value. Anyways I had managed to work out a solution that all parties would be happy with, it was legal and covered all compliance issues. Or so I thought.

Sitting in the boardroom with the NFP management team and the LSC sales people, I was ready to get the whole thing signed off and go to lunch to celebrate. The NFP guys were in total agreement and very thankful for all the hard work I had done and the best news was they only had to pay twenty-five per cent of what the LSC was demanding. It was a win-win situation – in my eyes anyway. The meeting basically broke out into a bar fight with the LSC sales people attacking me and then the NFP guys saying the deal was complete bullshit.

It was a little unexpected considering the LSC sales people's main focus was selling to and looking after charities and NFP's across the country. I had stupidly assumed they had similar values to me in working together to find the most cost-effective solution for the NFP.

How damn wrong could I be?

What it came down to was the dollars. LSC had a two million-dollar-plus target on the NFP I was assisting. Even more unexpectedly the lead NFP manager began telling the LSC sales people to basically, piss off and get out of his boardroom.

I sat there in that boardroom and watched the LSC people scurry out, I assume back to their gold plated, money-filled office towers and I thought, 'I accept there are these kinds of people who basically want to rip off organizations that are trying their hardest to support the less fortunate and the community.' The whole situation felt like a cash grab-and-run with no regard for the NFP.

It made my stomach churn, I wasn't sure if I was angrier at the LSC sales people for their greedy ways or deeply ashamed of myself for being part of corporate-land. I think in that moment I accepted I was doing the very best I could for the NFP but, I was done with toxic corporate-land. I knew change was coming, I couldn't hold it off. This scared me to my core or was it my status-filled ego hanging on for its life? This set off that stupid clown voice in my head shouting… *"How? How? How are you going to change?!"*

Honestly, I had no idea how… Divine intervention?

The great news was, after months of further work I got the whole deal signed off at the amount the NFP wanted to pay. They were forever grateful and for me it was like a massive "fuck off" to all the LSCs of the world; the little corporate guy doing the right thing *can* win. One for the corporate-hippy!

In the middle of that lesson I was having another: my sister had returned from Samoa and was in the final week of her pregnancy with her second child. I remember getting the phone call late afternoon from my mother.

"Your sister has just gone to hospital to give birth."

She tried so hard to contain her excitement and anticipation on the phone but I could hear it loud and clear in her frail voice and it still makes me laugh today. My mother loved a new-born baby beyond belief, it was frightening at times the love she would show to these new little people in a brand-new world. Maybe it was her drug of choice.

I somewhat shared her love for little people too, never wanting to grow up myself. I wanted to stay a child for the rest of my life. Kids have such a great energy and they are a great example of showing us what we all could be: free, accepting of all and with not a worry in the world. What I realize is that as we grow older we are all heavily influenced by our environment, culture, religion and now more than ever, social media. Sometimes it seems we're heading in completely the wrong direction if not actually regressing, as a species.

My mother called again and *BAM!* My sister had apparently fired out a healthy baby boy within minutes of getting to hospital. It blew my mind to think that she was in the midst of accepting a brand-new life into her world. I could only imagine what it would be like, to have created a life. I was anxious to meet the latest member of our family but I would have to wait till the next day.

I made my way to the hospital to meet my brand-new nephew, the Little-Guy. Bursting through the hospital's main entrance I was hit with that familiarly foul and memory-evoking smell but this time I just ignored it and powered on to find my sister and the Little-Guy. I walked into my sister's room to be greeted by what seemed to be an incredibly happy and joyous dead-looking person smiling at me. I paused for a moment… *Holy shit! It was my mother.* I had not seen her for a few days; she had just started some new cancer-fighting treatment and it had basically knocked the life out of her.

A little taken aback and shocked by her deterioration, I walked over to her and gave her a great big loving hug, ignoring the fact that she looked like *death in a dress*. I turned slightly to see my sister propped up in bed with the Little-Guy in her arms. It was a heart-warming sight. The look in her eyes was of total unconditional love and acceptance for an amazing new life that she had created. The Little-Guy was less than a day old and I was in awe of him, he was so tiny and fresh. This was truly an incredible moment for our whole family, especially considering what was to come in the following weeks.

What happened next was overwhelmingly emotional. My sister handed the Little-Guy to my mother. My mother then slowly shuffled across the room and sat down with him in her arms, her frail fingers gentle caressed his fresh cheek with loving tenderness. The look on my mother's face was one of so much loving acceptance for this new life she was holding, it was picture perfect.

This image is burnt into my memory; it was one of those "life moments" you don't often get outside of cinema, witnessing my cancer-ridden mother, with maybe only weeks to live, holding in her arms, a new life that was less than a day old. The situation made me literally step back and take in that moment of life's extreme contrasts. It was confronting, yet it was the day that I accepted the arrival of Little-Guy into the world and somewhere in my being I was starting to accept the fact that my mother was pretty much sitting in life's departure-lounge.

ЖЖЖ

CHAPTER 32:
CONNECTIONS AND UNCONDITIONAL LOVE.

So, with all this surrendering and acceptance going on in my life I was kind of starting to feel better health-wise, and to a point, mentally as well. I had been working hard with Guru-Guy to let go of shit that did not serve me well and I guess surrendering and having some degree of acceptance was a by-product of that.

I was learning and becoming more and more open to learning further. I started to recognize that the more I wanted to learn, the more lessons were popping up in my life. It's the old story of what you focus on, you start to see everywhere, and the mind is a powerful tool! I just wished sometimes I would use mine so much better to help myself and not harm myself but then that's all part of being human, or so I was learning.

It does blow my mind into tiny little pieces when I think from time to time what life shows you and what situations you end up in. The next few weeks were going to test me and stretch my emotions to levels I never even knew possible. Within all of that, they would teach me one thing that I will hold onto for the rest of my life. The essence of the human experience… unconditional love for one another!

It was around Easter time, the time to hang out with family, stuff yourself stupid with chocolate and generally have a good time together. However, it was the start of some intense personal lessons. Amazing too in some way but it would conclude with a very serious case of post-traumatic stress disorder.

I was happily pottering around my apartment, finishing off some painting when I got the phone call from my sister. My mother was in real bad shape and had had some type of negative reaction to the new fancy cancer-fighting treatment. So, it was paintbrush down and I was off to meet my mother and sister at the hospital to find out what the hell was going on.

Arriving at the hospital, or our family's second home as I was beginning to call it, it was the same old crap; trying to find a parking spot and then trying to find where in hell my mother was within the hospital. Being back there made me so damn anxious of what was to come and my head was racing.

"Is she going to die this time? Or is it just another false alarm?"

As I said before, the battle had been rough over the ten years. Not knowing most of the time what the hell was going on would set off my anxiety and I had had enough of feeling that way. I just struggled so much not having any control and more to the point not knowing what to expect next.

After about forty-five minutes I found a parking spot and then my mother, who was tucked away in a little room in the bowels of the hospital. She was all drugged up and looking closer to death than I had seen before. Surprisingly she seemed in good spirits and as always greeted me with her warm smile and a "hello love."

My sister was there too with the Little-Guy, he was fast asleep in baby bliss and none the wiser to the situation that was starting to unfold. I sat with my mother for a while, chatting about what had been happening with her and she went on to say she thought the medication was making her sicker, although she guessed the doctors knew better than her.

Mum had agreed (or I suspected she was basically forced to complete) her final chemo treatment due to being on some type of medical trial with the hospital or treating doctor. The little understanding I did have was that the final chemo treatment would lower her platelets to dangerous levels, which were already extremely low. Platelets are the things that basically stop you from bleeding to death – they thicken the blood.

At this point the doctor walked in and started throwing out all this medical information about my mother's condition: this thing was down, that thing was up. What I got from it was pretty much that my mother had no platelets left and she was on the wrong side of recovery. I remember thinking and then arguing with the doctor that her final chemo treatment would more than likely kill her. I was ignored.

The doctor went on to explain she was going nowhere fast and would be in hospital for the foreseeable future. It was back to the cancer ward for my mother with all the other cancer-fighting patients, some winning and some losing. I had kind of accepted that my mother's battle was quickly coming to an end and maybe from the very treatment that was supposed to heal her. I did let my thoughts known yet, I was trying to be super positive and have an attitude that all would work out fine.

How little did I know how it would all play out in the coming weeks… I did have that weird-ass feeling again, same as before my Mardi Gras debut, but for some reason I chose to ignore it.

So, she was one very sick lady, with life forcing her frail hand closer to pressing the doorbell to heaven yet she was fighting with all her earthly power not to do so. The energy in the room was thick with dread and I felt so damn helpless knowing I was unable to change the situation. The best I could do was to just be there for her. I could support her emotionally with loving care and that was about it. We all had to just hang on and hope for the best.

My mother was in the hospital for around ten days and in this time, I learnt more about life, connections with people, and more importantly my ability to offer another human complete unconditional love. I was still on light duties at work due to my sickness, which in turn gave me time to care and truly reconnect with my mother while she slowly wasted away in our second family home.

Every afternoon without fail I was by her bedside and stayed till she drifted off to sleep. In those days our bond as a mother and son strengthened beyond words. At times it didn't even matter that she had given birth to me, we were just two people on a journey that had total acceptance and unconditional love for each.

I was still quite sick myself yet, for some reason or the grace of God, I was there for her in my full capacity to serve her unconditionally. Most afternoons I would turn up in my designer suit with meals I had bought or made at home and try to feed her. I would clean her failing hands that were more like paws as time went on. I would wash her face most nights, very gently brushing her hair when she wanted it and I even attempted to clean her teeth with a cotton bud, trying not to choke her in the process. I couldn't use a tooth brush due to the risk of damaging her gums, her skin was like tissue paper and too much pressure or even a scratch could have made her bleed out.

I sit here writing this now and think back to how un-masculine it made me feel at times yet my identity at the time and my deluded bullshit lifestyle had little value and no voice while I cared for my mother. I didn't care what anyone else thought most of the time or said, and I honestly couldn't have given a shit how macho corporate-land viewed me anymore. I was a human being simply caring for another as I thought it should be.

The more I cared for my mother, feeding her, washing her face and hands or just spending time with her, holding her hand gently and talking shit or about her life and my childhood, the more it changed me deeply forever. It's hard to put it into words but, it was like a whole new part of me was being opened up and I was starting to see what I was capable of as a human being. Life, through this situation, was to show me how unconditional love and acceptance worked within me and also it brought out the endless compassion and empathy I could have for another. As screwed up and as bitter I was about my life, I was slowly beginning to soften up, by being shown how to be vulnerable with another without feeling threatened.

Doing what I was doing for my mother made me realize that we had in many ways dumped all our past misgivings towards each other and were in it together. The sad, or maybe very fortunate, thing for us both was that it took her to being on her deathbed and for me to finally drop my guarded ways, for us both to truly see each other. I think we finally both gave each other the space to be. To be who we were authentically after thirty-nine years. We are, or were, very unique people but in that time we saw each other with no conditions or judgments and it was something of such beauty. If only I could do this with everything, my life would be so different.

So, after thirty-nine years, what I saw in her was a soft, soulful and loving person who had set out in life with so many beautiful dreams and hopes of her own, just like I had. I saw in her a witty sense of humor – the small girl that had never grown up and the unfortunate pain of all her regrets.

I did seriously think, *Why the hell could she not have been this soulful person all of her life? Or why the hell didn't I see it before?*

It took this overwhelmingly difficult situation for her and me to let go and be true to ourselves. That was a massive lesson: be your authentic self, or at least try and discover it.

The most frightening thing however, was that I could see clearly now, even *feel*, her agonizing and complete non-acceptance for her impending death. We talked a lot about what might happen in those ten days and I let her know with the utmost empathy I would take every step with her. I think she was aware of what was going on but the fear of it all was really messing with her head. Still I tried so hard to calm her as much as I possibly could. The fact was, and as insane as it was, at some point in the near future she would have to make peace with herself and let go of life itself.

ЖЖЖ

CHAPTER 33:
SOME ROADS LEAD YOU HOME...

As time went on my mother's body slowly started coming apart, literally, right in front of all to see; her platelet levels had dropped to near zero. She was basically melting to death from the inside out. She was having more and more bleeds from the smallest of bumps and scratches. The doctors were finding it too hard to control the meltdown bleeds and the last few days she spent in hospital she was coming closer to looking like a mummy, the Egyptian kind.

The other three ladies in her room looked on in horror as they knew this could be them within a matter of months or less, if life chose to take them down that path. One of the women I chatted with from time to time was such a sweet person and it was her first time in the cancer ward for treatment. She had the unfortunate situation of being opposite my mother and got a 24/7 firsthand view of what may become of her. I wondered what the hell was going through her head while she watched my mother's body slowly coming apart right in front of her. Out of respect for everyone, I knew something had to be done; even more so to let my mother suffer in private to afford her at least some sort of dignity.

My sister and I met with the nursing staff and doctors to get my mother into a single room where we as a family could care for her without others having to witness the horrifying demise of a soulful lady. In the meeting the doctors advised my sister and me that there was no further medical action that could be taken. It was pretty much game over! They were going to try and keep her comfortable until someone answered heaven's door.

I remember sitting there with my sister in a consultation room while the doctors went over the details of what to expect in the coming days or maybe weeks if my mother was really unlucky. I say unlucky because if the family dog was in my mother's medical state, the "humane" thing would be to end its life due to the pain and immense suffering. At the time those thoughts rolled around my head, I was sure I could be the one to help my mother on her way.

How little did I know… I was going to find myself having to face this dilemma head-on in the coming days. Could I in fact do the "humane" thing and put my mother to rest or not?

…

We managed to get my mother a single special-care room. Once in her new room we had some time together and I explained what was going on in the most honest and empathetic way I could possibly find within me. Telling your mother that her ten-year cancer battle was coming to an end and all the little cancer-fighting soldiers had buggered off home was a massive dose of reality! For me it was the epitome of surrendering to what was. The situation brought my entire life to its knees in that moment, there were no more second chances this time around for my mum. Not a single person on the face of the earth could save her now. It was a nasty slap in the face: *"Wake up this is life Tim!"* Regardless of the God or the higher power I believed in, I was humbled yet devastated. More so for my mum.

Still she had little acceptance of her impending exit from this world. She lay there just staring into space with a look of utter determination on her face as though she was screaming at the soldiers to come back and fight. She then gently placed her paw-like hand on mine looking me dead in the eyes, "Get me out of this place, I want to be home… I want to be in my bed with my family around me." I could see cracks of realization in her eyes that her soldiers had left her and she was now standing alone on the cancer-battle field. She saw what I saw within her and she slowly turned her head and looked away. Again, she stared into thin air; I could sense the emotional overload in her as she sank back into denial.

I stood beside her shaking slightly, holding her hand gently with my head pounding of thoughts of her dying. "How would it happen? How will I feel and what the frickin' hell do I do next?" I quickly reined myself in.

Stay calm for fuck sakes, breathe… Breathe… Breathe! It's not about you right now!

I kind of snapped out of it. I looked straight at my mother and said, "Whatever you want mum, we will make it happen!"

I never thought such a simple last request would turn into a total nightmare. My sister and I met with the head doctor and administration people to get her moved to her true home, the home she had lived in all her married life. It was a place full of her beautiful and heartfelt memories. It turns out the hospital people thought it was all too hard to move her and it was in her best interest to stay put and die in an impersonal, sterile cancer ward. At first I was taken aback by their attitude and then the "whatever it takes" thing kicked in with me and even more so for my fired-up sister.

It got to the point where we both told the hospital people to go screw themselves and we would just roll our mother out by ourselves and hire some type of ambulance to get her to her true home. It was just mind-boggling that no one there seemed to give a shit about my mother's last wishes although it began to dawn on me that it was all about the legal bullshit. The hospital people did not want the responsibility of one of their patients dropping dead while in transit. It was too high a risk!

Within twenty-four hours, after a lot of demanding and at times shouting, plus a shit load of legal paperwork, my mother's wish was granted. She had legal sign-off to leave the sterile death-pit, to be with all her memories and more importantly, with her beloved family and friends in the security and comfort of her cherished home. It was like my sister and I had achieved the near fucking impossible; the relief and gratitude I felt welled up within me as a small tear popped out of my eye. My mother was coming home for the very last time.

This is where it got all a little too real for me. I was the one that had signed all the legal paperwork and was solely responsible for my mother while in transit. This freaked the shit out of me: I alone was going to be with her on her last ride home. The old head started spinning out of control with images of her dying in my arms while in transit or me totally losing my shit. Running man was screaming at me to *run, run, and run!*

It was heavy shit and a lot to take in then in when I was dragged off by a nurse to be shown how to administer all the hard-core-comfort-drugs to my mother once she was home. There were vials and vials of them, all to help my mother on her way to her next destination more comfortably. To be honest I had no idea what was what and when or how I should give what to my mother. It was a total head-fuck! I tried to reassure myself that everything would be ok and if things got too far out of hand I could always administer myself a vial or two and have a little lie down.

Once the "how to drug your mother" lesson was over it was time to roll the old girl down the hospital hallways for the last time to the waiting ambulance. Nurses and hospital staff seemed to appear out of a hospital black hole like seagulls spotting fresh chips at the beach; they had all come to say their final goodbyes. The goodbyes were intensely emotional, just as you see loved ones at the airport, yet here there was an unspoken acknowledgement that there was no return journey to this world. I watched on as person after person said their goodbyes to my mother. All of them had their own little way of saying farewell and I could see in their faces, my mother had touched their hearts with her soulful spirit. It was a very humbling experience to see the impact my mother had had on the lives of others.

With my mum next to me lying in her final hospital bed of this world, the staff slowly started pushing her out of her room and down the hallway to the waiting ambulance. It was like a ticker-tape parade with people on either side of the hallway getting in their final, final, *final* goodbyes and then one of the hospital people, I think it was the head nurse stopped us. She pulled me aside and handed me documents.

"These are the legal papers for the transit of your mother, it is incredibly important to have them on your physical body the whole time in transit, just in case something goes wrong." I stared back.

Holy shit…What does she mean, if something goes wrong?

One of the documents was a DNR order – *do not resuscitate* – which the family had agreed to and I had signed. I folded the documents up and put them safely in my back pocket.

Holy shit, what happens if something does go wrong and what the fuck do I do if she dies right in front of me mid-transit?

My "do whatever it takes" attitude slumped to the floor like an intoxicated teenage. I took a few steps back to my mother's bedside giving her a very fake "all is under control" smile and off we rolled to the ambulance.

The whole time I was trying to hold back the tears and keep my body from shaking with the fear of what might come. Maybe I should have got a DNR letter too for the transit. Holding onto the bedside to keep myself stable and upright, I talked gently with my mother, solely focusing on the excitement that within an hour she would be home, safe and surrounded by loved ones.

The hospital people loaded her into the back of ambulance and I wobbled nervously on board and took my seat next her. I very softly held my mum's paw-like hand for her last ride home as the doors slammed shut behind me. I had so much shit going on in my head from, "What if she drops dead?" to my old friend, "I want to run and I want run right now!" pushing me hard. I then realized I was locked in a metal box, in transit with no escape and my mother in a precarious state, wondering whether she'd make it home alive or not.

I thought, "I just have to do the best I can. For my mother's sake."

So, hand in hand we shared one experience on earth together that no one else could have witnessed nor passed judgment on, and this helped me to slowly drift back into a state of calmness. Together as we rode along the final roads to home, I peered out the little windows of the ambulance, giving a running commentary of all the landmarks as we passed them so she would know she was getting closer to the warmth of her own home. My mother lay there looking at me with a slight smile and eyes full of tears. While looking at each other I could see larger cracks of realization now in her face that her life was coming to an end, and I started to tear up too.

We made the final turn into our street; the street that she had walked us down so many times to school as a young mother and watched us play and ride our bikes as we grew up. Slowly the ambulance came to a stop and I could see my childhood home out the small window. It was like it was waiting with open arms to accept mum home for the very last time. What was to happen next was some kind of act of God or grace, again it was one of those "life moments" that is forever imprinted into my memory and brings a smile to my face every time I recall it.

The ambulance people slowly opened the back doors and as they did the calm afternoon sun gently shone in on us both, followed by a sweet-smelling cool autumn breeze. The only thing missing was angels with trumpets sounding the arrival of my mum. I was still softly holding her paw-like hand and we both looked at each other with a kind of a smirk and at the same time breathed out slowly. The look in the eyes of my mum was something between relief and gratitude that she was home: she was now exactly where she needed to be. As for me I was so overwhelmed with the whole situation I had pretty much forgotten about being relieved or whatever… I was busy looking for the angels.

As the ambulance people gently carried my mother from the ambulance to her final spiritual resting place, family and friends poured out of my mum's home to greet her. It was such a sight to see, so many people and so much love and care in the air. There were some people with the obvious dread of what was to come and I was one of them, of course.

When I do think back to our time in transit it feels like it was yesterday. In my head or maybe heart, it is the most authentic and humbling experience I have ever shared with another human being and for that I am so very grateful. However, no one and I mean *no one* on this planet could have prepared themselves enough for what was to unfold next.

Ж Ж Ж

CHAPTER 34:
THE FINAL BREATH.

Mum was now safely tucked up in bed in her beloved home and it was such a contrast to the sterile death-pit of the cancer ward. From memory it was a Friday afternoon. Looking at my mother lying in bed, with family and friends fussing over her was so damn heart-warming and I felt incredibly grateful for her getting her last wish.

The first full day passed with no issues at all; everyone was pitching in and helping out where they could. The place was starting to look like a halfway house with so many people visiting her and dropping off food or just turning up to see how they could help. Regardless of the situation emotionally and mentally, I remember feeling a strong oneness among all involved. It gave me a lot of faith in the human spirit.

Sunday morning I was sitting at her bedside as she awoke with a shudder, I gently rested my hand on her arm to let her know it was me. She turned her head and gave me the smallest of smiles and softly asked for some water. I had some water on hand and helped her as she slowly had a few sips. By this time, she had stopped eating and was high on all the comfort-drugs but surprisingly she still could put a few sentences together. She shuffled a bit to get more comfort and I could see on her face she was readying herself to make some profound statement.

This was to be her final wish from me, an impossible ask and a bone-chilling request that I had no idea how to respond to. With tears of despair rolling down her cheeks she began, "Please Tim, please do something for me, anything... I don't want to die, it's not right... I'm not ready, I want to see your finished apartment, I want to go back to Thailand with the family and I want to see the Little-Guy grow up... Don't let me die, please Tim. Don't let me die. Do something!"

With my heart in so much emotional pain and tears in my eyes, I lent in closer to mum with one hand on the side of her face and said in a very soft and compassionate voice, "All is o.k. mum, I understand and I'm here with you and I will do whatever it takes to care for you, it's all o.k. you just rest and don't worry about a thing, o.k.?"

Mum then sunk just a little further into the bed with comfort, my words had seemed to soothe her or it may have been the drugs, either way it felt she was in a nicer place. Her wish had totally freaked me out and I hoped that I had said what she needed to hear to give her some type of peace in such a devastating situation. Only weeks before I had finished reading a book on the theories, practices and process of dying from the Buddhist point of view. It was quite an eye-opening look into the process of death and how loved ones play such a vital role in assisting the dying through and into their "new life."

The thing that truly stuck in my head was to be very aware of my mood when in the presence of the dying. They may be completely out of it but they can still pick up on your energy so it was critical for me to be very calm, patient and full of unconditional love regardless of what was going on. The other thing was to give your whole-hearted permission to the dying that it was o.k. for them to venture off into their "new life" that awaited them.

It was one thing having these words and concept stuck in my head and an entirely different thing trying to embody them or even utter the words to another person, *"It's o.k. for you to die now."* It filled me with fear and utter panic. Yet I had to keep on realizing it was not about me, but about my mum, and I needed to step up to be at least one person there for her, fully present.

It was astonishing to find all of this within me and even more so to realize that I just got it and could get on with it. They say God, or whoever created us, will only put us in challenging situations that "they" believe we can handle, so that we grow. For me this was the definition of that, I was challenged to my limits and had growth spewing out every hole in my body!

The Sunday night I stayed right next to her all night as the others slept, it was another of those "life-moments" of which there were many that night. At her bedside I gently rested my hand on her arm or held her paw-like hand as she slept in a semi-comatose state. This is when I got the lesson on the importance of human contact very loud and clear. Without fail, every time I broke the physical connection with my mum she would wake and become very distressed until we reconnected physically and said calmly, "It's o.k. Mum, it's Tim… you're safe, just sleep mum… just sleep." And with a gentle touch and these soft reassuring words she would slowly drift back into comfort-drug-dreamland.

My mum was so panic-stricken with the fear of death and even more so about leaving the only world she knew behind. The fear of the unknown was seeping out of her soul and I could feel it through the physical connection we shared as I held her hand. It was like I was walking with her, holding her hand for security until she made it to the other side safely. I guess our roles had reversed, as a child she would hold my hand to cross the road or when I felt threatened and I was now returning the care.

I stayed most of the night with her holding her hand, if I wanted a smoke or to use the bathroom I would softly tell her what I was doing. Again, every time I disconnected physically with her, she would become very distressed and moan with fear. I left her bedside around five a.m. and went for some much-needed sleep as my brother took over at being the physical connection.

That Sunday night had such a massive impact on me and how I viewed the art of human contact, whether physical, emotional or spiritual. It blew my mind that me just being there holding my mum's hand would give her a sense of peace. The lesson for me was that when I'm in a calm headspace, one of empathy and unconditional love, my simple physical touch could make a difference to another human being. This was a very humbling realization; I would never have thought I had this in me. I guess the hippy was in play that night.

I woke that Monday morning with only two or three hours sleep and I knew it was D-day. The day my mum's life would come to an end after her well-fought cancer-battle. The first thing I did was to check on her and reconnect physically by softly laying my hand on her arm and saying, sadly for the very last time to my mum, "Good morning mum, it's Tim… how are you feeling?" There was not much of a response as she lay there motionless, it was as though she had slipped into another state and her breathing had changed to something of a sickening gurgling sound.

In the next hours Mum mumbled her last words to me as she drifted off into what seemed like a state of deep sleep. I continued to sit with her talking about the day, about life and then I stopped. I remembered that I had not given her my permission to die and from the Buddhist point of view this was a key point for the dying, so they knew it was o.k. to start their trek to their "new life."

Sitting there at my mum's bedside as she gurgled away lying on her side facing me, I leant forward putting my hand gently on her face… I took a deep breath slowly letting the air out and said with deep regret, "Mum it's Tim. All is o.k, Mum, it's time for you to go… you have my permission and it's all o.k.. O.k.?" I stayed in that moment with her for what seemed like hours just feeling and thinking the most positive thoughts of love, compassion and calmness. My body had other ideas as my heart thumped with physical pain, I felt sweaty yet cold but I knew I had to let her go whole-heartedly and give her the permission.

I slowly leant back with tears in my eyes with the realization I had just let go of the idea that my mum would live forever. She then moved ever so slightly, maybe a response to my words or she was acknowledging the fact I had let go and could feel that energy… I will never know!

What happened next has scarred me for life, with the never-answered question of... WHY?

I was staring at her face wondering what the hell was going through her mind when things spun totally out of control. At first, I noticed some blood slowly leaking out of her nose and with a more intense gurgle and a cough, blood starting spraying out of her mouth onto my arm and chest. In a state of utter shock, I just sat there staring at her as more and more blood flowed out of her nose and sprayed from her mouth. I tried so hard to fix the situation with what I had, only some tissues that were next to her bed. I didn't want to break the physical connection with her and I definitely didn't want her to know I was about to have a complete frickin' freak-out.

The running man within me had taken off in terror, screaming, and all my senses had short-circuited. I had the sickening feeling I was totally helpless to do anything for my mum. I turned away from her and softly at first asked anyone in hearing range for help and no one came. This panicked me even further, then I tried a little louder and still no one. I then basically shouted out in sheer emotional terror while having contact with my mum... "Please help me, can someone please help me!"

Finally, my brother and one of Mum's good friends who happened to be a nurse and an amazing lady to our family at this time (she was a total angel!) came racing into the room. They stood there in shock as they looked in horror at my mum. I was looking back at them thinking, 'for God-sakes do something, get me the hell out of here!' My concept of how the world worked had just exploded in my head and I had no understanding of why this was happening to my mum or why I would be part of it. In that moment life punched me in the face so hard I was losing touch of reality and I needed to be removed.

Angel-Nurse continued looking at my mum like she had seen that shit go down all too often. With a soft draw out sigh, she said, "I was hoping so hard that this would not happen." The tone in her voice was of total devastation. I was looking at the face of Angel-Nurse as she spoke, I could sense we were all in for one horrifying lesson of death in the extreme.

Angel-Nurse went into action to assist my mum and then me. I think my brother took over and I slowly walked out of the room, grabbed myself a coffee and sat outside smoking. I was so disappointed in myself that I let the situation get the better of me and I broke my calmness while in the presence of my mum in turn, no doubt affecting her.

I hated Mondays at the best of times but this Monday was going to be brutal one! My mum with all her strength, which I think was a cover for complete and utter fear, battled on. She was not going down without a fight, regardless of the outcome, so she bled and gurgled for the rest of the day and into the night. Every hellish minute felt like an hour as we all nursed her and tried to stop the never-ending bleeding.

I can't remember clearly if I had a conversation with my brother and sister or it was just one of those non-verbal I hear you eye contact moments. The bag of "comfort-drugs" was sitting on mum's dressing table close to her and I remember thinking or I may have said it…

"Surely someone can do the humane thing?" There was a deathly silence in the room as I think we all were thinking the same thoughts.

I was in total emotional numbness, just standing and staring at my mother, my heart racing. Then in my head a voice started justifying it like a rambling judge trying to make his point heard. I always thought I could have taken another's life, if it was necessary, due to extreme events. And this was beyond extreme. I was trying hard to give myself reasons why I shouldn't drug my mother out of her misery and the one thing that kept screaming at me was, 'I am not God and I have no right to take another person's life regardless of the situation.'

I couldn't play God, I couldn't drug my mother out of her misery, I had to just let nature or God do their thing and hope for the best outcome.

I was so damn frustrated by the situation and the inner conflict I felt was tearing at my heart, not to mention screwing with my head. I knew I couldn't live with myself if I did it; it was far too much responsibility for me to bear. I'm not sure what my brother and sister were thinking or were going to do, but I left the room again to sit outside, smoke and contemplate further if I had the balls to actually do it.

Sitting outside, it was a perfect autumn's evening, with clear, blue skies and the sun's light fading – it was so damn calming. It was such a contrast to what was going on just meters away as my mum basically bled to death. At least she was in her home and surrounded by loving family and dedicated friends. It was mind-blowing what some people did for my mum in her last days; everyone rallied around and took turns in nursing her. I never heard anyone say, "No, I can't do that," regardless of how grim the task was, everyone just did what they had to do to ensure Mum had the best care.

Walking back into her room I stood at the end of her bed witnessing just how horrific life can turn out. It was so confronting to look at my mum's bloody and now distorted face, it confounded any faith I had within me that there was a just world. My inner voice was just screaming, "Why? Why? Why?" She was a good woman; a church-going lady and she had a strong faith but on a physical level it seemed that this didn't matter. I just wanted to do something, anything, to help her move on to the next life. The whole situation was turning into something of a bone chilling B grade horror movie. My mum was starting to resemble a victim of a zombie attack!

I was starting to wish I had the balls to drug her; it was such a complex situation. As I said before, if she was an animal it would be the humane thing to do, to put her out of her pain and suffering. The conflict within me was chewing away at my soul, was I doing the right thing to just let nature take its course and be a witness to it? I still don't have the answer.

At about seven o'clock in the evening I went and sat with her again as Nurse-Angel gently soaked up the never-ending flow of blood. Sitting there I had the sense that my mum had left her body and it was only flesh and bone left. I could no longer feel the connection we once had; her spirit was gone forever, leaving behind only the mechanical motions of a human body.

I left her room in total numbness and despair that she had gone in spirit, the person that had brought me into this world was now in another. Nothing made sense in my head. My emotions were flying all over the place trying to reconcile with what the hell was going on and what had taken place. So, I sat with my brother and sister chatting about mindless crap for the next hour or so, as we all shut down emotionally and just laughed about the most, stupidest shit you could think of. One of which was watching the YouTube clip of *Philippines Got Talent,* the horse lady. Go figure... we all wanted to escape the current reality and this was the next best thing at the time.

In the mists of our emotionally moronic laughing fits I heard the faint voice of Nurse-Angel from my mum's room... "Quickly guys, quickly... Come, it's almost over." The three of us ran as fast as possible into the room. I remember literally bursting into the room, and it being quite dark and then I was over-powered by off putting smell. I guess it was the last moments of the physical body taking its last mechanical breaths. The smell and energy engulfed every last fiber of my being, and I didn't know if I was going to vomit, burst into tears or collapse on the floor!

For me it was an extremely intense moment as my head exploded into thoughts of, this is life Tim! *This is an amazing thing to experience, the passing of another to a new world.* Well on a physical level anyway. I had an uncomfortable sense of honor to experience such a thing, yet the pain of letting going of my mum was pumping through my body like fire. The reality of the situation lay before me, which was of true and utter physical devastation... my mum's cancer riddled body.

I leant forward and gently rested my head on my mum's side for the very last time, the last time of physical connection as I felt her slowly release her final breath for this world. The silence that followed was ear piercing and then I was overwhelmed with bone-paralyzing sadness which was overtaken by sheer relief that it was all over. The ten-year battle was done, I just wanted to slowly slide off my mum, onto the floor and lay in my shit storm of emotion until… Forever!

I was mentally, emotionally and physically stretched beyond my maximum limits as I stepped back and took one last look at my mum. Her face was distorted as though each and every cell of life had been sucked out of the back of her head by an industrial vacuum cleaner. The expression left on her face was of complete horror. I stood there staring at her face in total disbelief and then, I lost my shit like I have never before. Shaking uncontrollable and sobbing like a small child that had forever lost his mum in the supermarket of life.

I had thought about this moment many times and it had never occurred to me that it would go so horribly wrong like it had. I assumed she would pass gently and peacefully just like you see on the movies. I could not have ever imagined anything even close to what had happened in my wildest of nightmares. It was the most soul-fucking and horrifying experience of my life and somehow I knew I had to make sense of it all without despising the very creator of the situation… My then deluded concept of God.

ЖЖЖ

LESSONS LEARNT: #9

"Truly being selfless, putting my feelings aside for a moment and serving another in need unconditionally – left me a humbled man.

Humbled by the depth of vulnerability I felt and it is a 'forever' life changing moment – for with a vulnerable heart I got to experience unconditional love and a connection to life with another in that moment.

Now, that's living life!"

LETTING GO.

I left my mum's beloved home, the one of my childhood, and I knew my life would never be the same again. No more family Christmases, no more family birthdays and no more family dinners at home with my mum. I think driving back to my apartment I was in total shock at what I had just witnessed and that my mum had in fact just died. For some reason in my head I couldn't reconcile it. I had zero acceptance for her death and my idea of how my life was supposed to go was blown into a million pieces.

The whole time I was caring for my mum I learned so much about vulnerability and being true to myself. I experienced having her unconditional love and acceptance, and now it was all over. Now, the emotional pain felt like a hundred crazed rats digging their way through my chest, and the weight was unbearable… it was excruciatingly painful.

I don't know if you have ever witnessed death or for that matter the death of your mother, but I felt total loss and an overwhelming disconnect from my family history. My mum was the gatekeeper of family information and gossip; the gates were now locked.

Waking the next morning to a perfect summer's day just made it even more painful as I sat on my balcony with a coffee and smoke in hand staring into thin air, thinking what was next. The most fucked-up nightmare of my life was over but the funeral show needed to be booked and planned, the removal of my mother's 'material' life from her home and obviously the sale of it too. At that point my brain had a massive short-circuit, I guess a meltdown, and I went into auto-reboot coming to realize that the phone was ringing.

It was a family member telling me something about meeting a funeral person to start planning the upcoming show of my mum's last farewell. I had no idea what was even going on, what day it was or even year for that matter, I just agreed to everything and hung up. My phone rang a lot that day with people nervously calling me to show their respects or say how sorry they were for my loss. I knew I had to call others to let them know that my mum's bitter cancer-battle was over and I needed to inform corporate-land of my planned return date too.

Everything that I held so dear to me, my identity, status, career and the money seemed to be so pointless. It had all lost its value to me. I had the overwhelmingly daunting realization I had also lost my reference point in life. My mum was the one person on the planet I could call to ask those questions only a mother could answer and that was gone. It was as though for the first time in my life I stood butt-naked and alone on my own two feet knowing I had no home to go to. My childhood home was my home but without my mum alive and in it, it just became a house and only the memories of her there would lessen the pain of loss.

A few days later I found myself back at my mum's house with my sister and brother to meet with the funeral people and my old friend Mr. Minister. It was all too familiar, as though only yesterday I was sitting in the same place feeling the grief and loss of my little brother as we planned his funeral show. This time I was a little wiser emotionally and just let everyone have and do whatever they wanted to do. I basically sat back and agreed with everything, I had no energy and to a point no interest in the plans. This attitude did puzzle me though. I think I had spent so much time with my mum in her final weeks and days that I was done with it all.

I do remember thinking that I just didn't have the patience or the nerve to face other people at a very personal funeral show for my mum. The thoughts of my little brother's funeral haunted me for years; the biggest thing was being so emotionally raw in front of so many people. I had lost my head big time at my little brother's funeral while strangers peered into my world of pain and devastation like trespassers. That was one thing I never wanted to experience ever again.

So out of the funeral show meeting I had to sort out a photo of my mum, get it framed and ensure I turned up on time with it. My sister and brother had planned the whole show from start to end with slide shows, music, speeches and I think something about letting birds or balloons go at the finale. One thing we did all agree on was to play Kate Miller-Heidke's song "The last Day on Earth" at some point during the show which was rather ironic as I had listened to this song many times when super depressed and thinking of ending my own life.

I was still getting over my sickness and the phantom viruses that had played havoc with my body and to a point my mind. I think back and for the life of me I have no frickin' idea how I held it all together post-death and the months after. Well I think I did, yet I was later led to believe some thought differently... the beauty of perspective when in grief. Anyways the next few days I was operating in stunned-mode doing what I needed to do like a robot.

Much to my surprise a family friend had organized real-estate agent to meet with me and view Mum's house and in my stunned-mode I was just agreeing with everyone. My life was turning into one massive whatever! It was like three or four days after my mum's death and I was back at her house sitting in the living room as a real estate agent fired off question after question at me.

I remember thinking this is all too much, *What the heck am I doing talking to these people for? I need a drink or a good therapist at least.* Yet in my stunned mode I continued with the real-estate process regardless. I guess from the outside I looked like an unemotional freak trying to sell my mum's house while her body was still warm.

Then like magic I was morphed into a funeral setting and there I found myself again sitting in a church surrounded by some family and friends, but mostly people I really didn't know at all. This time though it was in a different church, the church we had all bid farewell to my father from, which felt like a lifetime ago. I sat there staring at my mum's coffin in what felt like a state of total numbness yet something inside of me wanted to scream the church down in anger. It was as though I was restrained in a socially acceptable straitjacket and all my emotions were trying to tear their way out like a crazed dog.

The funeral show went on, singing, speeches and a three minutes slide show summing up my mum's life. Then out of nowhere I needed to pee right then and there. Right at the front of the church I sat with hundreds of people looking on, I stood up and pushed my way past other family members to the aisle. The only way out was to go right past the coffin and use the minister exit and as I did I turned to look back on all the people bearing witness to my mum's final farewell. There were a few familiar faces as most looked at me with an expression of, *"What the hell is he doing?"* They were clearly wondering if I was o.k..

I burst out of the side exit of the church into brilliant sunshine and let out a massive gasp of air only to be greeted by even more fucking people staring at me like I was some escaping convict. So many people had come to show their last respects, I think there was more outside the church than in. I rushed off to do my business and then I realized I was obligated to return to the funeral show that I honestly didn't want to be at. I had said all my goodbyes to my lovely mum and she knew that.

I made my way back into the depressing and tear-filled church and took my seat with the remaining living family I had. A few people acknowledged my return in a sigh of relief that I had not done the running man and taken off yet, that was to come. Still feeling trapped within the situation of the funeral show I tried to get into it and think about my mum's tortured body lying in a box, pretty much right in front of me. I came up with... not much, no tears, no heart-wrenching loss like I felt with my little brother, I did feel slightly nauseous though.

The whole emotional thing was starting to freak me out, more so the fact that my body or mind or brain or whatever couldn't pick out a single frickin' emotion. I felt like an old malfunctioning jukebox trying desperately to select one song to play, but the song would play for a split second and skip to the next. I was at the point of having my emotions explode like a suicidal terrorist in a market when a family member gave me a shove to get up and do the final family hand-laying-thing on the coffin. That was then followed by the family walking slowly behind the coffin as the funeral people struggled to carry it down the aisle. This was the last thing I wanted to be doing!

This was when everyone could get a good look at you in a state of emotional whatever, I guess for me it was a deep internal meltdown brewing. I just wanted to morph the hell out of there ASAP! Yet I played my role like a good funeral boy participant. Once outside of the church we all bid my mum in a box farewell and then, holy shit! The "dumb shit people say at funerals" started again. And this was the last thing on the face of the planet I needed.

Some early-thirties guy that I had no idea who in the hell he was came literally bouncing up to me spewing out happiness and saying, "Wow what a wonderful day and what a great celebration of life it was!" He continued to verbally vomit out his happiness speech all over me. I took a step back from him, I think in readiness to punch him in the face, it was my fight-flight reaction to sheer and utter dumb shit people say at funerals. I gave him the smallest of smiles and without saying it but, sure as hell I felt it, I silently told him to fuck off and take his happy shit with him. I then took a very large breath letting it out slowly, kind of counting to ten to calm myself down in readiness for further uneasy people to offload their bullshit.

I gathered myself together somewhat and stood in my own space for a moment staring at the church with mixed emotions. I could feel my alert level rising to code red meltdown as more and more people kept coming up to me wanting to offload their prepared happy-or-sorrowful-bullshit-speeches.

It was like no one got it, no one could connect to how I was feeling and say the right thing to make all the pain stop, or make it better so I could make some sort of sense of what was happening. I just wanted someone to get it, and say the right thing to me, so my mind could select just one emotion and then I could move forward.

In my confusion and pain, I pretty much shut down and all I heard from others was… "I'm so sorry… blah blah blah…"

In all honesty, I didn't give a shit what anyone said, I just wanted to let go of everything, my life, the memories of what had happened, and the feelings of devastation and loss.

At that time I just didn't know how to, although I wanted and needed to let go of so many things in my life. But as I had learnt from Coach-Guy: you don't know what you don't know. What I do know now is that letting go in theory is all so simple, however, you need to be empowered to make the choice to do so in reality. The only empowerment I had was to punch people in the face. Anger issues much?

I came away from the funeral show a little bit angrier and more disillusioned with life, more so I think because of the bullshit games I felt forced to play in society. If I were truly honest with myself I would not have attended the funeral show, yet the pressure to do the "right thing" was too much to bear.

ЖЖЖ

CHAPTER 36

RESIGNING TO REALITY.

With the funeral out of the way life just rolled on regardless of whether I was in stunned-mode or code-red-alert for my pending mental melt-down. I was viewing my future as though I was standing on the edge of a busy freeway naked, having only just woken up from a deep sleep, and I needed to make my way across to the other side to continue my life. Everything was way too noisy, moving far too fast and looked too damn scary, so I basically turned around and ran the other way to hide out in the nearest bushes. I knew I had to face up to the reality of my situation, but I just didn't have the energy or the will to do so.

I needed to buy myself some time to work out what the hell had just happened to my life and how the hell I would move forward and get my head around where I was at. The other thing that was totally freaking the shit out of me was my growing awareness that my deluded identity, lifestyle and career had been devalued greatly through what I had experienced with my mum's death. I could feel life pushing and shoving me harder in a new direction, it was time to give myself some space to be.

A few days later I returned to toxic corporate-land and faced the cold-hearted reality that I needed time out. I also needed to inform Dog-

Man and Bald-Ego I was taking four weeks off. I called a meeting with them both and honestly I never saw anything like what was about to be unleashed on me in my entire life. It was the *"What the fuck moment"* of 2010 in corporate-land!

So, I was sitting in the boardroom feeling like total shit, like someone please shoot me in the head to put me out of my misery. Looking like death warmed up on a stick and still mostly in my stunned-mode, Dog-Man and Bald-Ego walk in. Dog-Man sits to my left and Bald-Ego sits opposite me on the other side of the boardroom table. I start out with a little background story letting them clearly know what had happened on the family front, that my health was still not good and I was basically not coping, I was burnt out.

I went on to state that I was taking four weeks off to sort out my health and some personal family issues and to take time out was incredibly important me; I needed it. In all honesty and possibly stupidly, I showed both of them my vulnerability card in a hope they would understand my situation further as you would assume a decent human would. This is when the shit storm unraveled into something of a "lamb to the slaughter" situation and I was the lamb!

Bald-Ego leant back in his chair, his arms behind his head and he had a look in his eyes of "I smell blood and I know where I'm getting my next ego feed meal from." That would be me… and then he kind of swooped forward at me from across the boardroom table like some massive eagle coming in with claws out to devour his prey. So, it was official, the shit storm had started.

He went straight in for my ego jugular… "So you call yourself a sales person, do you? You call yourself a businessman? You can't have four weeks off! What are you totally stupid? It's eight weeks till end of financial year and you want time off! Are you a fucking idiot?" He went on his egotistical rant for about ten to fifteen minutes as I just sat there looking at him.

I was a little stunned, yet it kind of washed over me like when you're very drunk and you piss on your shoe accidentally, it's no big deal. I think Bald-Ego could have beaten me with phone books or with a bag of oranges and I still would have just sat there looking at him.

I was so over the corporate-land bullshit and games. I could see through it all now and more importantly his little man games. I had just showed up as I was: no games, no bullshit and no fear, and I had stated where I was at in corporate-land and what I truly needed. Simple you would think!

His rant finally came to an end but the most surprising thing was, or maybe not, Dog-Man just sat there, didn't say one word, no support or buy-in. I gathered my thoughts together in my head and I slowly leant forward and very calmly suggested to Bald-Ego that he could stick my career up his ass.

Now I was empowered, not to punch anyone in the face but just walk away like a good hippy boy. It was such a massive realization that I just didn't give a shit any more about my identity or deluded status that I had worked so damn hard for. I had just realized that it had zero value!

In that moment, I went to get up and leave, Bald-Ego's whole attitude changed into a very passive one. Suddenly it was "no need for you to leave, we can work something out" kind of deal. Within that moment I had thoughts of, *What the hell am I going to do career wise and for money?* Yet a sense of peace bubbled up within me telling me that there was nothing to worry about. I had a freaky knowingness that someone was looking out for me and I just needed to do what I needed to do. So, I kept moving to leave and then Bald-Ego demanded I sit back down so I did, I had nothing to lose.

As I sat there looking and listening to Bald-Ego rant further on how he thought I was over reacting about leaving, I noticed he was kind of nervously laughing as he spoke. I think by telling him to stick my career up his ass and then getting up to leave I had called out "bullshit" on his first ego-rant. I had basically punched his ego in the balls and knocked the wind out of him, he had to match my attitude or lose.

I learnt that day that if I'm authentic with myself and back myself up while in a state of vulnerability, which is not being weak, just being honest and open to what I honestly needed with others, it kind of melts the others' crazed ego bullshit. I stood my ground and we managed to work out a plan so I had my much-needed break without both of us erupting into an ego fueled corporate-land battle.

I walked out of that meeting and corporate-land feeling a little happier with myself, yet Bald-Ego had added further bitterness to the contempt I already had for him and for the whole of corporate-land. As for Dog-Man, my manager, and the one person who should have either stuck up for me and or had my back, just sat back and let me get devoured. So, in my mind I had pretty much resigned that day, regardless of what I had or hadn't agreed to with both of them.

I guess the day I let go and let myself be authentic and vulnerable in front of others within corporate-land was a massive thing. Doing what I did was so damn empowering, I knew that I could now walk away from my career, corporate-land and to an extent my deluded identity.

It was the knowledge of this that drove me, even excited me, to push my life into the unknown of something better. I had a four-week pass and I was going to get the most out of it. First up I needed the help of my remaining family to sort Mum's house for sale.

Then I was running and as fast as I could away from all the shit that had happened. I needed some serious alone time to process the first quarter disaster of 2010. I ended up putting the house sale thing on hold and opted for the running and run I did... straight to Bali for ten days.

ЖЖЖ

CHAPTER 37:
ME TIME...

I decided to spend a few nights in the mountains of Bali and then five nights down by the coast... *Get me some beach, sand and sun!* I was thinking this would be the perfect balance and was hoping this would help me gain some equilibrium in my own life, or at least in my emotional state. I can't express enough how happy I was to get the hell away from all the shit that had just happened. The feeling of escaping it all gave me cool and calming shivers all over... I was officially on the run!

How little did I know that I would end up dragging all my emotional crap with me to Bali. There was no escaping it unfortunately and I found that out the hard way when I arrived at the hotel in Ubud, a beautiful town in the middle of the island. The hotel was about a thirty-minute walk out from town on the side of a mountain in the jungle. It was very secluded and peacefully connected to nature. I was taken to my room which felt like a three-hour walk through the jungle along paths, down stairs, back upstairs, and then along another path before finally arriving at my room, which was an old-style Balinese design. It was a little dark and had a funky smell about it. I flopped onto the bed and thought... *I can just relax and watch some shitty cable TV, pop a sleeping pill and then slowly drift off to sleep.*

I loved nothing more when on holiday than to watch shitty cable TV and eat junk food lying on the bed. I had the junk food, the bed and as I scanned the room… *Holy shit… No frickin' TV!* I turned the place upside down like a crazy man looking in every possible place I imagined I might find one. None was to be found anywhere. At this point I think I could have killed someone. I just wanted to watch something to chill out and numb my mind.

At the prospect of not having a TV, my mind and emotions went way out of control, part panic attack yet more so reliving my recent past. TV was the drug I needed to stop me from thinking about the things I had tried ever so hard to leave behind. But I had not succeeded; they were firmly wedged in my forehead and were coming with me wherever I went. The faster I ran, the more they would wobble around slapping me in the face.

I lay there on the bed stunned and sweating. I had booked a hotel without a TV… *What the hell had I been thinking?* The silence was deafening, apart from the frenzied sounds of the wildlife outside my room. It felt like an act of God that I had no TV… It meant I had no way of escaping my emotions. I was condemned to be alone in my room in silence with them and this just freaked the shit out of me! I was in escape mode; this was not supposed to be 'let's face your demons' time.

The good news was I had brought two books with me. One was about eating and praying and the other was a book of short stories on people's experiences with death. Not sure why I had these books but that was what I had. The alternative was to think myself into a crazed state. It really felt like life was doing its old thing of shoving and pushing me in directions that were anywhere but where I wanted to go. I was a little bit aware of this but still I wanted my shitty cable TV.

After a few hours of sweating and freaking out I started to read the death experience book and, *damn*, I connected to the stories instantly! I should have been reading it at my mum's funeral; it just seemed to press the right buttons within me and with this some sense of understanding of what had happened. Knowing that other people out there were experiencing the same feelings comforted me in my non-cable TV room for the next few nights.

The other thing that I thought would maybe ease my emotional turmoil was to see a fortune teller. I was hoping they could give me some kind of insight into the way things were, as well as to my future. The next morning I walked into the center of town in search of one. I asked in several shops, but no one seemed to know what I was talking about let alone have any idea where to find one. Wandering down the street feeling a little defeated I noticed a tourist information office. I would give it one last shot and if all else failed I'd go have a massage.

I asked the woman at the desk if she knew of a fortune teller and she looked at me blankly. Then her face lit up. "Oh… You want to see the medicine man!"

She proceeded to give me directions which sounded like something out of *The Lord of the Rings*. Leaning towards me and speaking in broken English, she softly said, "Listen very carefully, go to the old central market, turn right and follow the winding road down to near the monkey forest. Turn left at the old banyan tree, then take your first left, second right and there you will find him." I was not sure how to react to that! I felt like laughing, thinking, *Lady, are you fucking with me? Is this a joke?*

She disappeared behind the counter and then popped back up with a business card in her hand. She went on to explain how the old medicine man could read your soul and had healed many people in her family and the community. I was thinking, *hmmm… this is not what I was really looking for.* Yet something told me to go check it out anyway.

I thanked the woman for her help and off I went on my not-so-certain quest to find a medicine man near some monkey forest by a banyan tree. I was still in two minds as to whether I should go or not and continued walking around the town center. I stopped for some water and a smoke, sitting on the side of the road. Out of nowhere a taxi driver startled me by asking what I was looking for and where I wanted to go. I must have stared at the guy for minutes while I tried to work out what the hell to say. My inner hippy was like, "This is a sign, show him the card and go see the Medicine-Man." I thought a little longer on what I wanted to do, concluding with, *Fuck it!* I turned to him and said that I wanted to see the Medicine Man. I showed him the card and his face lit up like a Christmas tree! He looked at me with excitement. "Oh he is a great man, a healer of many. He helped me and my wife to have many children when we had problems. I will take you there right now."

Before I knew it, I was in his taxi and off to see the Medicine Man. I had nothing to lose and everything to gain and I just hoped that what he had to say would make some type of sense to me. Arriving at the Medicine Man's house, which was more like a compound, I followed the taxi driver through an old Balinese stone archway into a courtyard which had a large kind of worship structure in the middle. The courtyard was surrounded by three, maybe four, small buildings which were also in a Balinese style. It was a little dark and damp yet the whole scene had a calming effect on me, which was enhanced by the sweet and distinctly Balinese smell of fragrant incense burning.

Off to the left sat the Medicine Man, on a wooden balcony in front of one of the small buildings. He was partly surrounded by what looked like large bookshelves packed with paper scrolls. Everything looked aged and rustic, including him; as though he had been sitting in the same spot healing people for hundreds of years. It all felt a bit mystical.

He was deep in conversation with a Western woman, holding her hand as they sat there together. Suddenly he stopped with the awareness he had visitors. He turned and looked at me and the taxi driver standing in the courtyard. He spoke brusquely to the taxi driver in Bahasa before immersing himself once more in deep conversation with his guest.

I was taken a little aback by his abruptness as the taxi driver ushered me out of the courtyard and back onto the street. He assured me that everything was o.k. and I needed to come back the next day at three thirty p.m. He drove me back to my cable-TV-less hotel, chatting the whole time about how the Medicine Man had changed not only his life but also the lives of many of his family members. I was feeling a little excited, maybe even more so curious, as to what the Medicine Man might tell me of my future. But I would have to wait.

I returned the next day. My head was still out of control as I walked nervously through the stone archway into the freakily peaceful courtyard, full of anticipation of what was to come. Medicine Man gestured for me to come and sit with him on his wooden balcony with open arms and a big warm friendly smile on his weathered old face. I sat down with him on the floor with the old grass mats gently scratching my legs as he leant forward and grabbed my right hand quite assertively.

Sitting only a few inches apart, he looked at my hand as I observed him. I was trying to work out what the hell he was about and how old he must be. He looked well over a hundred, with eyes that were a foggy brown color and only a few teeth left. The most striking thing was that he had such a calming effect on me. Tugging at my hand for me to move a little closer to him, he grabbed my face and looked into my eyes, apparently scanning for something. It was as though he saw right into my soul and I could feel it. It was rather off-putting to say the least. Still staring into my eyes, he suddenly demanded to know why I wanted to see him.

I was a little stunned and before I could reply he let out a groan of acknowledgement. "You have much pain in your life. You are a real man, an honest man and a decent man, but you need to protect yourself!" With his other hand he started poking me in the chest and then himself several times saying. "Ah we are same-same, we are very sensitive men, same-same."

I was a little unnerved by the pokes, thinking, *O.k. cool, Mr. Medicine Man, relax… enough with the poking!* He kept on insisting that we needed to protect ourselves, as we could both pick up on other people's negative crap and we had to be strong. He also told me that my life partner was coming and that I was about to receive a lot of money in the next few months and I needed to fly, fly like a bird!

We chatted for over an hour about life, my future and interestingly about him and his life. I was totally captivated by this old guy. He told me he had been a medicine man all his life, like his father and his father's father. All the paper scrolls surrounding him were from them and had been passed on down the line. There must have been hundreds of years' worth of information sitting in front of us. His life, from what he told me, was overflowing with human experiences, from wives he had outlived to healing many, even meeting a very famous Hollywood actress.

I asked further about the actress and he had no idea who the hell she was, but he said many fancy American people had come to film him with her for a movie. He thought it was all too much of a fuss, the simple life was much better for him and he liked it that way. Then he told me I must go and see him in the movie… He let out a big laugh and said, "I'm famous!" We both looked at each other and laughed with an unspoken understanding that being famous was bullshit.

He was such an interesting human being, with so much life knowledge and wisdom. You could really see it in his very being. His humor was great too and I felt we both had a strong connection, he saw me for who I was and just got me as I appeared. It was just what I needed;

it kind of lifted me out of my crappy emotions and made me feel somewhat alive again. Happy, even!

I walked away from the experience with Medicine-Man feeling so damn accepted and understood, just as I was. It seemed to flick a switch on in me, of hope and that everything might work out o.k. in the long run after all. I wondered around Ubud that afternoon seeing life a little more positively. I had the old skip in my step back and could feel somewhere in my emotional crap my smile was coming back.

One thing that stuck in my head that he said was, "Fly... fly like a bird!"

Shit yeah... I was going to fly... fly like in a plane out of my old life to other country once I had sorted out the sale of my mum's house! Just as I thought that, I was engulfed with fear of change yet the thought of flying away gave me goose bumps with excitement.

Damn I was confused! Was I becoming bi-polar too?

I had more time to process my confusion in Bali as I relaxed and sunbaked by the beach. It did dawn on me again, if not for the thousandth time, that for change to happen I would have to let go of what I thought I knew and most importantly let go of my screwed-up status. I still had massive struggles with it all and this would rumble around in my head like rocks in a clothes dryer for weeks, if not months, to come. I sensed, however, that if I didn't make changes or let go, life was going to slap me around again. You would think I would have been a little more up to speed with the way it all worked by then, but I wasn't. Life had its hand poised ready to give me yet another slapping around!

ЖЖЖ

LESSONS LEARNT: #10

'Knowing when I have hit my limit and 'enough, is enough'.

Then to take full responsibility of me and my life to ensure I am aware, balanced and empowered in what I think, say and how I react.

Only I can do this and that's through my absolute 'commitment' to self first so that then I may be able to serve others authentically."

CHAPTER 38:
THROWING OUT MEMORIES.

Arriving back in Australia from Bali I felt somewhat refreshed, but nonetheless overwhelmed at the realization that firstly I had to face up to a few facts. I had just turned forty mid-flight; it was the middle of winter and freezing and I was effectively an orphan that had yet to pack up his mother's life. I still had two weeks before returning to corporate-land to face its bullshit, so I had a little bit of time to readjust and get things moving on the sale of the house.

Health-wise things seemed to be improving and Bali had done me the world of good... Thank God! So, I ploughed headlong into the sale of the house, thinking all would run smoothly. How little did I know what a shit fight this would turn out to be, to the point where it almost totally screwed up my relationship with my sister and older brother. I think one of the main problems was that we were all so exhausted emotionally and probably suffering from post-traumatic stress disorder from our mum's horrific death. We all had very different views on what we should all do in sorting out our mum's personal belongings and estate. This was a perfect recipe for a massive disaster and a grueling family feud to boot.

Having much more time on my hands and being the "Type A" guy I was, I planned out the whole pack-up-and-sale in detail with spreadsheets; the lot. I had timelines, target dates and lists of who would be doing what and how. My inner control freak was in full swing, I was not so aware of this at the time. However, it would become apparent to me with time. I met with my sister and older brother to run over the plans, thinking it was fair and just for all involved.

How damn wrong was I? The calm meeting I had imagined got way out of hand. No one could agree on what to do and my plan turned out to be flawed... It was way too much and all too soon. We were all still very emotionally raw and trying to move forward at this point for my sister and older brother was far too soon. I needed to get some closure around my mum's death and I guess doing what I was doing was the vehicle for that: face it... pack it up... sell it off and get the hell out of there! The whole time I could hear my mother's voice in the back of my head, continuously repeating, "Just get it done... Just get it done!"

However, my sister was trying to adjust to her new life that had begun with the birth of Little-Guy just months earlier, before watching her mother basically melt to death right before her eyes. She didn't want to let go of the house, which I totally understood. Unfortunately, I lacked the words to articulate my understanding to her and the fact was, if I had stopped for one moment to be present about the house sale I would have imploded with grief! I was hell-bent on moving forward at any cost to save myself from facing my feelings. I think my older brother was in the same state as my sister, plus he was too busy with his family and career to give the time needed. That is, the time I needed from him, to do what I needed him to do to push forward, so we could all move on with our lives.

I was trying so hard to do my best yet my intentions became completely misunderstood, especially in the state we were all in. It was a very emotionally charged situation, trying to sort through a loved one's material life not knowing what to keep or what to let go of. Every time I walked into the house I would get the cold sweats and have flashbacks of what had gone on just weeks prior.

It scared the shit out of me to even be in the house alone but, I sucked it up. I was on a mission.

One thing I did learn while packing up my younger brother's apartment after his suicide was that it was the best therapy for me. To be surrounded by his personal stuff eased the pain for some reason. Not sure if I understand that one fully but anyways it helped me. With that, I just pushed on and started sorting out my mum's personal stuff and by doing so the therapy process started again. I ended up staying at the house for days on end going through every item my mum had ever owned. The whole time I was talking to her out aloud as I slowly unpacked cupboard after cupboard of her life.

Looking at all the stuff she had in her house, I'm sure she was a borderline certified hoarder. The best thing was all the crap she kept from our past, which was astonishing; it brought up so many happy memories that as a family we had all once shared together. You name it, she had kept it. There was shit shoved into the back of every cupboard in the house. Every room was like its own mini time capsule. I even found gifts that I had given her dating back to the 1980s which made me laugh out a lot. I could hear her voice in my head saying, "Waste not, want not... Timothy!"

Unfortunately, we wasted a lot of her things in the end, throwing out years of her material life. It was heartbreaking to do it but we couldn't find a new home for it all. My sister rang so many different charities and most weren't interested in anything, it was either too old or too much of a hassle for them to take. I guess we live in a throwaway society these days and I could sense my mum turning in her grave with all the things we had to throw out. With the house mostly cleared of her stuff it was time to do the unconceivable thing and put her beloved home up for sale. As the magnitude of the event began to sink in, I couldn't believe it had come to this; it was like selling part of my childhood.

ЖЖЖ

CHAPTER 39:

THE LAST PROMISE.

Before putting the house up for sale, I had one last thing to do; a very important thing. I had promised my mum several times months before she died and before I got very sick that I would fix up and paint the interior of the house. This was satisfying therapy for me to finally deliver on my promise before selling the house. We had talked about colors for each room and at the time her color selection was questionable yet I just agreed with it to keep her happy. I did change some colors but more importantly I kept my promise to her, dead or alive. I worked my ass off to fix up and painted almost every room. Again, the whole time I did it I talked to her, telling her what I was doing and how the painting was going. This process gave me so much peace and kind of took the edge off the grief.

While in 'my process' and being so focused on keeping my promise to my mum I had basically ignored my sister and older brother. My relationship with them broke down to the point of despair. I could barely manage my own emotions and trying to think of others at that time was beyond my capacity, which just fueled our insane situation into a 'he said, she said' shit-fight. Looking back now, we were all so very fucked up and trying our best to hold off a complete emotional family bleed out.

In my wounded state, I saw it as though my sister and old brother had turned on me. We were all on very different pages and I was doing my very best with what I had and knew. This just added so much more pain to the situation and the more I tried to fix it the worse it got, to the point where I lost total understanding of why we had all even started fighting in the first place. It was a total mess, a nasty place to be in with the people I loved: they were the only immediate family I had left. I had that shit feeling I had lost control of my being and my life was rocketing in a direction of… "Here comes another cruel and bitter life lesson!"

In my attempt to deal with the situation, I think I may have thrown them out along with most of mum's material life too. I was on a roll and anything I deemed to have no use or that didn't fit anywhere, and I couldn't find a space in my wounded world for them to occupy. I guess I just shut down emotionally as well; I had nothing left to offer anyone, nor myself for that matter. The challenge was I still needed to deal with them to get the estate finalized and the house sale day was swiftly approaching! I would have to face them in person at some point, as I was pushing on with the sale of the house, doing what I thought was needed.

So, I was in what felt like a never-ending shit storm, the running man within was screaming at me daily, like propaganda from loud speakers to get the hell out of there. The urge to follow this advice was so damn strong it took all my mental strength to stay put until sale day when I could sign the paper work, get my cut and run as fast as I could.

I had no idea where the hell I was going to run to, but when a dreamy voice started in my head, saying over and over "South America… Go to South America Tim." Regardless of that, I felt even more pressed to get out of the current situation and Australia for that matter.

Finally, sale day came around and I had to face my remaining family at the house. Despite the need to get it done, I just wanted to crawl in a hole and die but this was something I had to be part of. The day was shitty, the sky was overcast and not exactly ideal weather-wise for a house auction. Nonetheless, it took place in the backyard with fifty or so people turning up along with the real estate agent and the auctioneer. Sitting in the back room with my sister and old brother reluctantly present, I stared out the window at all the people. It was so surreal to see so many strange faces standing in our backyard, the same backyard that I had spent most of my childhood digging holes in or setting fire to stuff.

It was brain-numbing that the place where I grew up was about to be sold to the highest bidder and within weeks I would never be allowed to return to it. I had a moment of, what *the fuck are we doing? We can't sell our family home; I need to stop it!* I broke out into a clammy sweat and then was startled by the loud bang of the auctioneer's hammer and heard the words, "Let's get this house sold today!" It was all too late, I just had to sit back in my sweaty state, suck it up and watch.

As the first bids starting rolling in a truly magical, if not divine thing happened, just like in an old Bible story from my childhood. As I stared out the window in despair at all the strange people vying for my mum's beloved home, the clouds seemed to slowly part as rich, warm rays of sun shone down, lighting up the whole backyard. It sent goose bumps racing from my toes to the top of head, it looked like Jesus was about to be beamed down from the heavens. I turned apprehensively to my sister as it all happened and smiled, we both sensed right in that moment that mum was with us and she was giving us all her blessing to sell the house and move on with our lives.

We both had tears in our eyes, I had no idea how to react but, I felt like sliding down onto the floor, assuming the fetal position and having a good old fashioned sob!

The great news was the house sold for a lot more than we had all hoped, which in a weird way seemed to excite us all. Once the sale was complete we met the happy new owners. They were a couple in their late twenties with two small kids and the freaky shit continued… the wife was so much like my mum, right down to her mannerisms. Not only did she look like mum, but she had a similar style of dressing too. It freaked me out! I could see tears in her eyes of happiness and what seemed like relief now that she had a home for her kids.

Standing there chatting away with her I couldn't help but feel these were the right people for my mum's beloved home. It would once again serve another family, creating new memories over time, just as it had for my family for the past forty-four years or so.

Leaving the family home that day knowing it was all over and there was no turning back left me somewhat empty. However, looking around the house with all its freshly painted walls that I had done warmed my soul. I had kept true to my promise with my mum, sadly a promise she would have to witness from another place.

ЖЖЖ

CHAPTER 40:
FACING THE BITTERSWEET FREEDOM.

With the death of my mum and ensuing sale of her home, I was given three things… One was the devastating realization that I could never go home again, which freaked the living shit out of me. For the first time in my life I had no parents, no home and felt totally lost without them, it was like I had a massive disconnect to my past. The second one was that it gave me a lot more money. It made my bank account look so damn amazing. The final one was that it gave me the freedom to empower the running man within me; I now had the means to let him run pretty much anywhere he desired.

The whole situation confused the hell out of me though and I looked at life with an attitude of, *what the heck was that all about? And, how the hell did I get here?* I had gotten my freedom: no more torturing thoughts or feelings of when Mum would die and how the hell I would handle it, or wondering what we would do with her stuff and the house. I had no more responsibilities to look after her and no need to worry if she was ok. It was done. Finished. The ten-year cancer battle was over! The most confusing thing was the price I had to pay to get to a point in my life where I had a feeling of freedom. It was the epitome of the double-edged sword and I struggled to make sense of it all.

I may have been beginning to feel free and my bank account showed me I could up and run at any time but I had one last responsibility left in my life: corporate-land. Running man within me was still screaming his lungs out at me to run as quickly as possible away from my past and my deluded lifestyle. Life was about to show me very clearly what I needed to do; it was the last piece of the bittersweet freedom puzzle. Life was about to shove me in the direction I needed to go.

A few weeks after the house sale, the final ass-kicking piece of the jigsaw was revealed. It was not going to be pretty, and I was going to revisit the past all over again: enter potential cancer battle number two. I woke up one morning feeling like total shit, my previous sickness was back with a vengeance. I was sicker than I care to remember. It was the same everything, in every way, but tenfold. I felt overwhelmingly defeated and was raging with anger at life. I couldn't understand it, *why the hell was this shit all coming back? What other bloody lessons did I need to learn?*

I went back to see Doc-B and it was all the same tests again and then the waiting game for the results. I knew how it worked but do you think I could control my paranoia or my patience? *No...* I was panicking the whole time of what it might be, constantly thinking of the worst-case scenario.

Days later I got the results back. Doc-B seemed more concerned than last time as he went through all the results with me. Then he came out with those words again, "It doesn't look good Tim, all indicators are pointing to Lymphoma again... I'm sorry." I sat there staring into nothingness with deafening silence ringing in my ears. Slowly thoughts started getting louder in my head as I focused back on Doc-B's pity-filled face. I knew what he was going to say next and I didn't want to hear it but I had little choice in the matter. I was back to the cancer-clinic to revisit my nice Cancer-Doctor.

Going through the process again and knowing full well what I was in for. I think most days I sat shaking my head at what was going on with my life, it just all made no sense. I saw the nice cancer doctor, again going through all the tests and then it was more damn waiting for the results.

With the "Day of Doom: Part Two" approaching I had all the old thoughts again. One new one was, *had I dodged a bullet last time or had the doctors missed something? Was I actually slowly dying after all?* My paranoid state of mind was seriously running riot, I had no control by the time D-Day arrived. As for my anxiety... it was off the scale!

There was some good news, I had managed to patch things up to a point with my sister and she had insisted on coming along to support me, which was great. I needed some support. I found myself sitting in the cancer-clinic waiting again, thinking and pretty much freaking out. I was finally called in to see the nice cancer doctor: same room, same everything but this time I kept my mouth shut and just let her talk. Again, I had the same results with the added extra of, *Wow! An additional unknown virus floating around my system.*

I was then palmed off to the special infectious diseases unit for more tests. The great news was I had no cancer, the bad news was... the doctors had no idea what the hell was wrong with me. I'm not sure what is worse. Having cancer that at least has a chance of being fixed or no one knowing what was wrong and having no frickin' idea how to fix me. It was a total head-fuck and added to that I was slowly losing my cognitive abilities, my sight and my memory. Feeling as though at any moment I was going to drop dead, I just gave up and went with the flow of it all.

ЖЖЖ

CHAPTER 41:
THE TURNING POINT!

A week later I meet with the head professor of the infectious diseases unit after even more tests. I was told I had what seemed to be post-viral chronic fatigue syndrome. The reason why I was losing most of my bodily functions was the viruses had affected my brain which in turn had enlarged and basically my body had had enough. There was no quick fix, or any fix really; the head professor had seen several cases like mine and most of them were dying just down the hallway from her office.

To be honest, in a weird way I was so happy to finally know what was going on with me, in spite of there being no immediate fix. Just to know what I had gave me a little peace and I felt that maybe I could somehow fix myself with time.

But there was more… The head professor demanded that I rest as much as possible and not be in any stressful environments whatsoever. I looked at her thinking, *yeah right… how the hell do I do that?*

And this is when she delivered the final piece of the puzzle. She leant forward and looked me dead in the eyes and said with a very stern voice, "If you do not change your lifestyle immediately Tim, I can pretty much guarantee you, you will be sharing a room with the dying within months!"

She went on to say that my condition was life threatening and I had two choices: change or get even sicker and die! I slumped forward and put my head in my hands staring at the floor. My heart felt like it had stopped and I could barely breathe. I was overcome with the feeling that my whole deluded life had just come to a bone-rattling stop. I could see it all exploding into a million pieces. Life had basically served me notice; I was being evicted and I needed to find an entirely different lifestyle to inhabit.

The situation just freaked the living hell out of me, confusing me even further. My mind started playing ping-pong with the idea that I could have my deluded lifestyle but I would die, or I could kill it off and live. I know the answer looks damn obvious but, well, it was my identity! I left the head professor's office with the ping-pong game playing at full speed. *Should I change or not?*

The ping-pong game went on for days in my head until I was notified that the money from the sale of my mum house was in my bank account. It was an emotional moment; I was so damn happy with what this money could do for my life yet felt very uneasy with the price that had to be paid for it by all. I logged onto online banking just to see what my bank account looked like and I must have stared at my balance for hours. I now had enough money to do whatever I wanted and it felt overwhelmingly amazing!

Then I had an intense realization I needed to make the decision to change my life for the better. I remember sitting at my computer in a cold sweat, feeling like my head was going to spin off into the abyss. I had every reason in the world to change my life and now the money to support it. I could easily continue as normal and then use the money to pump up my deluded lifestyle but I would have to then face the consequences that that would have on my health. This didn't seem to feel right. Then it struck me. *I could use the money and my savings to buy life experiences instead of more materialist objects.*

Without a doubt, that simple thought changed my life forever! It felt like something of a divine intervention… I took a deep breath and made a commitment to myself to change my life right then and there. *This was it!* It was as simple as that, I sat back in my chair thinking how damn easy it was to make such a massive decision. I felt kind of lighter, like someone had lifted a bag of cement off my head.

Life in its crazy ways had put everything in place, and I was the one getting in the way of myself, or more so my egotistical mind. It was now up to me to listen better and be more aware of what life was offering me. That day I surrendered to the cold hard facts that my time in corporate-land, along with my lifestyle and career was all over. It was an incredibly liberating experience to finally let go and have some sense of knowing I was going to be o.k. even if I was losing the identity and status that I valued so highly. The great thing was, I started having more insights into what was else was important to me and what I needed to do began to just flow effortlessly.

ЖЖЖ

CHAPTER 42:

THE GREAT ESCAPE PLAN.

For years while working in corporate-land I had dreamed about escaping it all, even making some failed attempts. I remember in my early twenties daydreaming of just taking off, leaving it all behind to explore the world and experience different cultures. It was hard to believe that I was about to fulfill those dreams and even harder to believe I had the cash to do it. Regardless of my health issues and all the adversities of my past, I felt so damn grateful that finally I was in the position I was. Finally, I could set running man free!

So, my plans... I had been thinking things over for quite some time even though I was so unsure what the hell I was doing. I guess somewhere in the back of my head I knew I would take off to newfound lands. For some reason, deep within me while thinking about where to go and where I would be the happiest, South America kept popping up again and again.

I had to take into consideration my health and thought about whether I could in fact travel more adventurously or if it was best to go sitting under a coconut tree for six months. I had further meetings with Doc-B and we discussed health-wise what would be the best options. We both ended up agreeing that it was not important where I went as long as I got the hell out of my current situation and made time to rest and heal.

With that in mind I thought, *Fuck it!* South America it was. If it didn't work out, then I could…well make it up as I went along. Just the idea of getting on a plane and getting the hell away from my deluded life was inspiring enough. I was also fooling myself to a point. I thought at the time to escape my situation was going to ease all the bullshit in my head. Basically, I was trying to run away from myself… This would come back to bite me on the ass, but for the time being I was so unaware, and I honestly didn't give a shit. I was very much focused on my amazing life travelling around South America.

South America was very special to me. Ten years earlier I had spent three months in Peru where I had just connected to it like no other place before. I also met some beautiful soulful local people and I had promised them and myself I would return one day.

In my head I could see clearly a map of South America and a travel route of where I wanted to go. I spent hours online looking at every possible travel option but nothing seemed to match. I was starting to get a little frustrated with the whole thing and then my sister said I should check out a travel company she had once worked for. I checked it out online, scrolling through every page to the point of giving up until *bam!* I did one last click on a page and up popped the exact map that had been in my head! Yep… it was a *holy shit* moment. To make matters even more amazing, the tour started on the exact dates I was looking for and it was right on my budget.

As I said before, once I had made the decision to change my life things just happened; everything in my life flowed with ease. I did think, *Why the hell didn't I start doing this earlier?* It all seemed so simple: surrender to what is and go with the flow. I still wish I could remember that on a day-to-day basis!

I rang the company, booked the tour and paid for it right there and then. The tour was a four-month overland journey around South America starting in Santiago, Chile and finishing in Quito, Ecuador. Now there *was* a catch, or at least a concern for me. It was with twenty to twenty-eight people in a truck and most of the time we would be camping.

The other concern was that I had to sort out how I was going to get to Santiago. I also needed to decide what I was going to do with my apartment, car and all my other personal crap that I had thought was so important. Oh, and then there was the simple matter of how I was going to finalize things with corporate-land. This one stressed me out somewhat.

I was still sick but with every day moving closer to South America I was fighting harder and harder to feel better. It was surprising how having a light at the end of the tunnel changed my whole view on life; it just made me feel that much better. I manage to sort out all my travel plans and first stop was Buenos Aires for ten days for some much-needed Spanish classes. Then I would be off to Santiago, Chile to start the tour. As for all my personal crap, I thought I could just sell it all or give it away; it would be a therapeutic detox for a once materialistic guy.

The apartment I decided to rent out for a year and hoped like hell that was the right thing to do. The whole time I was making plans for my great escape I had to ignore the nagging voice within asking me, 'What are you doing with your life? Is this right? You're making a huge mistake!' It did my head in and at times confused the hell out of me but, I kept my eyes forward and focused on South America.

ЖЖЖ

LESSONS LEARNT: #11

I found this out the hard way!

"With no intentions, plans or actions in my life, I was going to end up 'somewhere' with stuff and people I didn't really want."

CHAPTER 43:
BYE-BYE CORPORATE-LAND…

I had scheduled a meeting with the Smiling-Assassin. He had been the one who had given me the opportunity to join the company, so I thought it would be best to tell him first that I was leaving. With what had gone on with Dog-Man and Bald-Ego I had no time for them and I was still somewhat bitter. They were my direct reports but I thought, *fuck it, they will find out in due course.*

As it turned out the Smiling-Assassin wanted Bald-Ego in on the meeting and so there it was. We met early morning in Smiling-Assassin's office and both men had a look on them that I was up to something that was not going to benefit them. I guess I had the upper hand in this corporate-land game after all, I was choosing to walk away and risk it all; it was game over!

I told Smiling-Assassin that my leaving date was the twelfth of November. His first response was, "I *so* knew you were going to do this." He said it with a smile on his face yet, I just felt under that smile, he was thinking, *"You shit-bag Tim!"*

Bald-Ego just sat there with his mouth open, somewhat in shock. I think he was freaking out that I was taking my shit and leaving. Bald-Ego was responsible for all the sales targets and ensuring the sales team was performing. I held a lot of the knowledge, delivered on targets and knew the systems inside out. Bald-Ego was counting on me to prop up Dog-Man's lack of experience. He finally spluttered out some words, something along the lines that I couldn't leave, asking what I was doing this for.

Before I had gone into the meeting I had got it clear in my head what I was doing. There was to be no revenge or playing games with them, I just needed to do what was best for me for once. Through the whole thing I only wanted to part ways very professionally and ensure I did the best I could do regardless of what they thought and what they wanted to do to me. Again, for some reason the whole process just flowed. I did all my knowledge transfers and handovers to management with no problems or bullshit. I tried not to give too much away regarding my future-plans, only saying I was taking a year off to recover and rethink what I wanted out of life. In all honesty in my head I had plans only to travel around South America and then see where I ended up.

The surprising thing was so many colleagues and clients were very excited and happy for me, most of them saying they wished they could do the same. It was very touching and inspired me further in creating this new life for myself. Then there were those who totally disagreed and made it known. I got the whole range from, "You're totally crazy, you're throwing away your career and your life," to, "Your decision is very stupid and you will regret it, how can you walk away from your career and life?"

One thing I did learn is that there is so much importance put on status and identity; what you have and what you do rule in corporate-land. The sad thing was, who you are does not count for much at all but that was the very thing that was becoming more and more important to me. I think when you're forced into focusing too much on the other things, it clouds the very essence of who you truly are and you lose yourself. Well, that was the case for me anyway. Maybe I am truly blessed that life forced my eyes to be opened.

So, with corporate-land sorted out and an end date fixed, I nursed my ailing career to its final death. Well maybe not death but, for me something died within me in the last weeks of corporate-land. It was a very weird experience to stop my career after fifteen years and change direction to become a travelling nobody. As I said, over time my career and corporate-land had become who I was, and on some level I was now walking away from myself.

This was scary as hell but also so empowering. Just the thought of it was somewhat inspiring. I was forced into a situation and I was taking control of my life in a very positive way to finally look after myself, regardless of what others thought.

And this was a major step forward for me, given that previously, what others thought about me was my black angel of stress and worry; it would unwind me every time I entertained it. But for some reason, this time, I just did not care what others thought. Then on my last day in corporate-land I was thrown a massive curve ball by Bald-Ego. I used to stress so much over what he thought of me, of course it was always negative and this used to drive me totally crazy. So, on my last day the management team, much to my surprise, wanted to have a farewell gathering for me, which included all of the staff.

Quite honestly I just wanted to say a quick good bye and get the hell out of there as fast as my legs would carry me. I didn't want any farewell, drinks or pats on the back but management had a different plan for me. So, at five p.m. on my last day I was called to the boardroom and confronted by the whole company for my final goodbye to corporate-land. This is when I experienced: *A whole lot too late.* Bald-Ego got up the front to speak on behalf of the company and went on to praise me for all my hard work, saying how I was one of the cornerstones of building what the company was today.

This guy had given me seven years of ego attitude, torn me down in front of colleagues and called me so many unfavorable things and now I was a cornerstone of the company! I stood there listening to his praise and looking at him with my mouth on the floor, thinking, *What the hell are you going on about? Wow, this is too much too late mate!* I must have been in shock at this point as the whole company cheered and clapped once he finished his speech. Then I was put in that shitty situation of having to respond to his speech in front of the whole company.

I just stood there for a while laughing nervously as all of them just stared at me. I knew what I wanted to say in that moment… 'Thanks Bald-ego for all your bullshit over the years and I think you are a total douche-bag with an over-sized ego, which matches your fat, shining head.' But instead I took a deep breath thanking everyone as I realized I was not so angry any more, all the bitterness seemed to just melt away with the one simple thought, *in less than 30 minutes I will walk away from all of this, never to return.* This gave me so much peace, all my bitterness and evil thoughts of anyone involved disappeared. My inner hippy was finally happy!

Dog-Man wanted to have a final word too and went on about how he agreed with the Bald-Ego and that I would be missed around the office. Especially my humor and infectious laugh. He handed me a present and everyone started shouting "Open it! Open it!" So, I opened it and it was a *Mont Blanc* pen. I thought, *what the hell am I going to do with this?* Imagining myself backpacking in South America writing postcards with a four or five-hundred-dollar pen, it made me laugh out loud, much to the confusion of others. In that instant, I thought I could E-bay it, just as Dog-Man said, "And we got it engraved with your name on it." I was like, *oh shit! No selling it on E-bay. It's coming backpacking with me!*

Straight after the farewells Bald-Ego ambushed me in the hallway and starting going on and on about how we could work something out for my return. He basically stated whatever I wanted he would be happy with, I could work from home or in the office, whatever hours I wanted and he wouldn't change my salary or conditions. Again, it was too much, too late. I told him politely I would think about it but for the time being I needed to rest and recover… *Oh and get the hell out of there!* It was like finally he had realized what I had achieved and how valuable I was to the company and for that moment I saw Bald-Ego as a decent human being.

I walked out of corporate-land with some form of pride and knowing that people valued me and notice my efforts, regardless of all the bullshit. Driving home from corporate-land for the last time, I seriously thought I was going to explode with joy! I was a free man after fifteen years of crap and I was still alive and kicking, albeit somewhat mentally and physically fucked up from the experience. The best thing was that for the first time in my working life, I did not need them yet they were begging for my services. Somewhat egotistical I know but, *what the hell!* It felt great to be wanted by corporate-land and still to just simply say no thank you and walk away from it all. It was the most liberating thing I had done in years… if not my life!

ЖЖЖ

CHAPTER 44:
ACTIVATE THE ESCAPE PLAN.

T he next morning waking up, it was a Saturday and *holy shit!* I was a free man. I lay in bed for a while contemplating the gravity of what I had done and what lay ahead of me in the coming months. The sense of relief was overwhelming; I had cool chills all over as I felt released from corporate-land.

Of course, my egotistical mind was beyond despair with the worry of what might be but I just told it to shut the hell up. I was officially on a mission to somewhere now; I was not sure where I would end up but at that point I didn't really give a shit. All I knew right then was I need to activate the last part of my escape plan and get my ass to South America.

I had about a seven-week countdown to pack up my materialistic life, sell it all or give it away or stick it in a box. Oh, and rent out my apartment. It was game on! I also planned a week or so in Thailand with my sister's family and some friends, which I was so looking forward to. What I wasn't looking forward to was my first Christmas without a mother or a family home to celebrate it in. The 'no mother, no family home' thing played heavily on my mind. "Where the hell would I go for Christmas? And whose family would I spend it with?"

Just the thought of it made me want to run screaming the other way. I did not want to face it at all.

I tried to stay focused on what I needed to do and that was enough to distract me for some time. Letting go of all my material stuff I had once valued even more than myself was so damn therapeutic. I think most of my stuff had been bought mainly to impress others and show off my status, this I was starting to discover about myself. I came across items that I once loved or maybe coveted yet, being a little further in touch with what was very important to me, they seemed to be somewhat worthless now.

Within two weeks I had sold or packed away my materialistic life almost completely. Only the shell of it was left and surprisingly I felt so damn calm about it all. The even more surprising thing was my health was improving daily and I was becoming a "letting go" junkie. I was loving the feeling and the process of what I was doing.

I remember standing in my apartment looking at the bare basics of what was left of my old, life just before the real estate people turned up to view it. I had, well, mixed emotions; some regrets that my life had not worked out as I had expected it to but the most overpowering feeling was utter, deep-seated gratitude for what I had once had, and for the mind-blowing opportunity to walk away from it all. I was starting a new life and would potentially travel the world with next to no responsibilities.

It was an intensely humbling moment; I wasn't sure if I was going to laugh or break down into tears of joy!

Then I was jolted out of all this by the loud buzz of the intercom. It was the real estate people coming to view the apartment and so that I could sign all paperwork. I took a risk and rented out my apartment for one year partly furnished in the hope that within that year I would work out my true life-purpose, or at least some kind of plan for my future. As I signed away my apartment for the year my paranoid voice returned, wailing, "What are you doing? What if this or that happens? What the hell are you going to do then?" I ignored it and pushed on. It was now official... I was to be homeless within a matter of weeks and there would be no turning back.

I was left with only one backpack weighing around thirty kilos which was literally stuffed full with personal belongings for my South American adventure, plus one daypack for all my camera gear. That was it. From corporate-man with a loft apartment, sports car and a deluded sense of status, to a man with two bags and a desire to run! But the man with two bags had the world at his feet and could do, see and be anything he wanted. I only realized this once I was in Thailand sitting with my sister at a cafe and she said... "This could be any cafe in the world and you can see them all... in any country you desire... can you imagine that?"

I sat there for a while imagining all the different places I could see, meeting new people, trying different foods and learning new cultures. I was overwhelmed with excitement and a sense of freedom that I had never experienced before. It felt like having a full body orgasm from the tips of my toes to the top of my head. It was utter bliss! I did have to keep realizing my new reality and that corporate-land and the old life was just a memory.

Adjusting to my new life was a day-to-day process and I had no idea where it would lead me but it felt like I had started something that would never finish. The hardest thing was getting my head around the fact that I had no mother and nowhere to call home for Christmas. As I said before, I viewed Christmas as being fairly special to me but that Christmas I could not have given a shit. I just wanted to speed up time and be on that plane to South America.

I did ending up having Christmas with my sister and her in-laws which was o.k. but lacked so much compared to the warmth of the Christmases of years before. Actually, it was fairly depressing. Most of the time I stood or sat watching the others doing their Christmas thing. I had the realization repeating over and over in my head, *nothing will ever be the same again*. It didn't matter how much I wanted things to stay the same or people to stay in my life. The cold, hard facts were that people die, things change and life rolls on regardless. I just wished I could have let go and rolled with life on this.

I would be letting go of more things as well: my attachment to the country I lived in with all its social and cultural values, my friends and my old ways of living. I was fairly sure I could roll with that! I was so ready for a new start, to be shown a new outlook on life and just do things differently. I wanted to explore and really find who I was underneath all the crap of who I *thought* I was, and more to the point, who I thought I was through the eyes of others. I was embarking on the adventure of a lifetime with no real time frames or defined outcomes. To be honest it felt like I was truly entering into an abyss compared to my tightly controlled and planned corporate life.

It scared the life out of me! However, I was starting to like the idea more and more.

With the escape plan activated and only a few more things to do, like say my goodbyes and hand over my apartment, along with what was left of my materialism. The final day in my apartment before leaving to stay the last few nights with my sister was a bit of a non-event. I looked around it, I think trying to get emotional for the last time and say my final goodbyes to one of the major pieces of my old deluded status, but there was nothing, no emotions. I simply grabbed my two bags and walked out with the door slamming behind me. Then I stopped turned around and looked at my front door thinking, *what the fuck? I feel nothing, no attachment... Nothing?* I opened the door and had one last look and it just looked like an apartment I used to live in, that simple.

The escape plan was now complete and I could now make my way to the departure gate! Well, not quite. I had the last few nights staying with my sister and then it was...

"Please make your way to the departure gate!"

ЖЖЖ

CHAPTER 45:

THE DAY OF THE GREAT ESCAPE.

With all the goodbyes and farewell drinking done, it was the day of the great escape… Wednesday the 12th of January 2010. This is a date that will stick in my head till the day I die. That day I left behind the delusions of my old life: the life that I had desired so much and worked so damn hard to obtain. In the end my desire for the holy grail of status was for me ultimately empty and had nearly killed me.

It's funny, not to say totally ridiculous, what we sometimes fight so damn hard for only to realize once we have it, it's not what we wanted nor is it even healthy for us. I was happy to leave it all behind, try somehow to make sense of it all in a different environment and I hoped to God that I had learnt from it.

Arriving at the airport with my sister and some friends, I was now merely a man with two bags and a one-way ticket out of everything I thought was so important to me. I had pretty much broken free from what I thought society and others demanded of me. I could not help but feel utterly liberated and all the bitterness I had felt about corporate-land was gone! They could be swimming in their current but I was happily floating downstream in mine.

With that thought I ever so slowly floated over to the check-in counter and checked in my bag. It was all so surreal when the woman said, "And here is your boarding pass for your Buenos Aires flight." I thought I was going to explode with excitement, I could smell South America and feel the warmth that I had experienced ten years before.

I basically skipped, hopped and jumped over to where my sister and friends were sitting and told them I better get going to board the plane. We said our final goodbyes and had a hug and I walked off. I was thinking, *that was all a little weird and far too easy*. I knew I would not see them for months, possibly years but I honestly had no emotional response to the situation or them.

As I waited in the line for immigration and security, I couldn't make sense of how I felt about leaving the people I loved and cared so much for behind. I think it was all too much for me emotionally so I unconsciously convinced myself I didn't need anyone in my life and nearly shut down emotionally. Also, the fact running man had taken me over and was firmly fixed on getting on that plane to South America and the fuck out of Australia! The whole situation was completely different to what I thought would have played out. I thought there would be at least tears or some heartfelt words… it's funny how half the time what you expect is not reality!

I cleared immigration and security with no problems and made my way through the consumer paradise that is duty free shopping. I checked out a few things and wandered around waiting for my flight. I did start contemplating the lead up to me being where I was in that moment and how I felt. The conclusion was: *Stop frickin' thinking. Sit back and enjoy the ride of your life Tim!* Which was fair enough, I did think far too much. In fact, to the point where I lost track of time and had to basically run to the boarding gate.

Before I knew it, I was sitting on the plane as it bumped and rattled its way to the runway for take-off. I was staring out the window saying my goodbyes to my motherland thinking, *Holy shit… I have really done it; I have done it… there is no turning back now!* I couldn't believe I was on my way to South America, I was like an excited kid on the verge of peeing his pants. Then with a jolt and the plane came to a sudden stop and didn't move any further for about thirty minutes. Finally, the pilot advised us that the plane had technical problems that he couldn't fix from the cockpit and we would be towed back to the boarding gate for repairs.

Seriously? You've got to be shitting me! I think I actually said that out loud as other passengers looked at me with faces of… well, total agreement.

I'm not a good flyer at the best of times and this information freaked the hell out of me knowing full well we would be flying over water for most of the flight, plus it was a twelve-hour flight. That pretty much killed the kid in me: there was no peeing any more it was more like I was about to shit my pants in paranoid fear! We were finally towed back to the gate for repairs which took two hours. In that time, I had convinced myself the plane was going to crash land into the ocean and we all would be eaten by sharks. By the time we were again bumping and rattling our way back to the runway, I had popped a few sleeping tablets to calm the nerves so I was more than relaxed and ready for take-off!

As the engines roared and we shot down the runway I looked out the window in my drugged state and gave my life and my motherland a final wave goodbye. I was now in the air and on my way to my new life's great unknown adventure.

In retrospect, I had made so many poor choices and could not have got it any more wrong than I did but to be where I was… IT FELT SO DAMN RIGHT!

ЖЖЖ

THE END.

To be continued…

LESSONS LEARNT: #12

"Sometimes the smallest step in the right direction ends up being the biggest step of your life.

Tiptoe if you must, but take that damn step and enjoy it – because it might be your last!"

LINKS AND REFERENCES:

www.dallaszoo.com/wildlife-conservation/conservation-partners/
dian-fossey-gorilla-fund-international

www.eckharttolle.com

www.mitchalbom.com/d/books/3856/tuesdays-morrie

www.thesecret.tv

www.alanwatts.org

www.brenebrown.com

www.mayaangelou.com

www.startwithwhy.com

JOIN THE MOVEMENT!

Corporate Hippy
R-evolution

'Sharing Lessons Learned'
Awareness | Balance | Empowerment

The Mission

*"Influence and 'empower' people, executives and corporations
in making 'balanced' choices with 'awareness' for an improved and sustainable
life
experience for One Million individuals by 2020."*

@ Facebook: Corporate Hippy R-evolution
www.facebook.com/groups/CorporateHippyRevolution

Get the Moaching and Courses: www.corporate-hippy.com

EXTRA

The Three Questions:

"Only deal with the truth when answering"

1. What is it that I am doing that is currently working?

2. What do I need to stop doing that is getting in the way of what I want?

3. What do I need to start doing that will empower me to move forward?

AVAILABLE
15TH ARPIL 2018!

A series of short books on practical solutions to life's madness, for super busy and stressed people who desire more balance and peace in their day-to-day lives.

THE
LITTLE,
HUMAN
HANDBOOK

Series – Volume One

Awareness | Balance | Empowerment

Volume One: Awareness, Balance, and Empowerment. Practical solutions on understanding yourself better and why you do what you do. Improve how you manage your life's stresses and struggles on day-to-day bases, and then doing your 'thing' in a more balanced and peaceful way with passion.

For further information click here

www.corporate-hippy.com

THANK YOU!

Thank you for reading and I trust you enjoyed the experience!

Would love to here your feedback.

Please leave a review on Amazon, Facebook and share with family, friends and colleagues if you think it would add value to their lives.

Thank you for your support!

Web: www.corporate-hippy.com
Facebook: @corphippy
Facebook Group: www.facebook.com/groups/
CorporateHippyRevolution
Instagram: corp_hippy
Medium: www.medium.com/@tim.a.mcmahon
YouTube: Corporate Hippy
Email: Hello@corporate-hippy.com

I also offering services focused on
Awareness | Balance | Empowerment

Public Speaking
Moaching - Coaching and Mentoring
Business and Sales Consultancy
Courses (The C-GAP Project)
Online Courses
Workshops
Retreats

Please feel free to sign up for further details @
www.corporate-hippy.com

Printed in Poland
by Amazon Fulfillment
Poland Sp. z o.o., Wrocław